Robert F. Suczek

THE
BEST
LAID
PLANS

 Jossey-Bass Inc., Publishers
San Francisco · Washington · London · 1972

THE BEST LAID PLANS
A Study of Student Development in an Experimental College Program
     by Robert F. Suczek

Library of Congress Catalogue Card Number LC 72-5891

International Standard Book Number ISBN 0-87589-149-7

Manufactured in the United States of America

JACKET DESIGN BY WILLI BAUM

FIRST EDITION

Code 7234

The Jossey-Bass
Series in Higher Education

Consulting Editors

JOSEPH AXELROD
*California State University, San Francisco
and University of California, Berkeley*

MERVIN B. FREEDMAN
*California State University, San Francisco
and Wright Institute, Berkeley*

Preface

This is a book about human change, about people beginning with definitions and metaphors, using them, and then changing their definitions. *The Best Laid Plans* is about changes resulting from an experimental teaching program, the first attempt to establish an experimental college program at the University of California, Berkeley, in 1965. The program was an effort to develop an alternate educational plan for the first two years of college. The story of the experiment is a story of teachers changing their views of students, of education, and of each other. In the course of working together to realize their ideals about education, the direction of their expectations and of events frequently did not coincide.

The initiation of the program marked the beginning of a period of reevaluation and change in higher education, a movement which has not spent its force. Residential college programs, cluster colleges, colleges without walls, contract programs, as well as varied curricular and teaching innovations, are being developed in increasing numbers. *The Best Laid Plans* is directed to those engaged in efforts at educational reform such as these. Much can be learned from this educational experience. I hope the book will provide direction for others engaged in similar projects.

Paralleling the interest in educational reform is an interest by psychologists in the study of personality development of college students and the effect of various forms of higher education on that development. *The Best Laid Plans* is based on research which was a part of that psychological interest. The research began as an attempt to study the differences in the personal development of students in the experimental educational program and in the regular undergraduate program. It was designed in the tradition of previous research in this area, a tradition that stresses rigorous scientific method. Personal observation is acceptable only as a preliminary procedure, awaiting the development of systematically applied quantitative measurements. The research is designed to establish a stable reference point against which change can be gauged. The intent is for the researcher to liken himself to an observer motionless on shore, watching and evaluating the progress of a sailboat along the horizon in relation to himself. The intention, however, was not realized in this study. As the complex nature of the two educational structures (experimental and regular) and of the developmental process unfolded, the original point of view of the research was no longer tenable. Research questions and research method changed. It became evident that a qualitative appraisal was more appropriate than a quantitative one. The account of these changes belongs in the stream of work dealing with the effects of educational programs. It is directed to those doing such research as well as to those who use the results of studies for planning and evaluating educational reform.

Young men and women were the subjects of the study, which focused primarily on the way they experienced this period of their lives. In the quantitative measures and in our direct experience with the students in the experimental program—in periodic interviews and in discussion groups—some of their ways of experiencing life, of changing, and of remaining the same became evident. The account of these ways of change forms the largest part of *The Best Laid Plans.*

Student development emerged as a research problem much more complex and difficult to study than was anticipated. The students were growing, developing young men and women, and their development was connected in varying degrees to aspects of their situation in life: their families, their peers, the university, their teachers, and the educational structure. The nature of the connections was only sometimes evident. An additional complexity was the fact that the process of change going on in the individual was accompanied and complicated by accelerating social changes. This factor influenced not only the students and their attitudes about their own development but the problems and methods of research in this area.

A consistent observation throughout the study was that everyone involved was changing: the student engaged in his life in college, the teacher in developing a new educational form, and the researcher in learning about the other two. A principle that emerged from these observations forms a basic theme of *The Best Laid Plans.* The process of action based on engagement in a task provides the context for change. That principle leads to one of the conclusions of the book—namely, that the point where teacher and student interact with each other must be the concern of educational process and structure and also of the researcher interested in observing change in and development of students.

In the development of the study on which *The Best Laid Plans* is based, I am much in debt to a number of individuals who have been colleagues and are my friends. Elizabeth Alfert, research psychologist, took responsibility for major aspects of the work and acted as my assistant and collaborator throughout. She literally was the staff of the study. The study owes much to her resourcefulness in dealing with problems of data gathering and analysis and to her imaginativeness in perceiving the implications of our observations. For me, the constancy of her position about theory and research method was most helpful when my own thinking was yawing wildly and threatening to swamp the project.

My colleague and friend of many years, Harvey Powelson, director of the Psychiatric Department of the Student Health Service, encouraged my undertaking the study and was the official participant observer in the Experimental College. His unofficial participation was even more important to me and the study: his patience in hearing out my ideas, his astute observation and criticisms of them, and his own reflections about the students and processes we were studying. His insistence that I look harder or look again at some conclusion I had drawn contributes much to what fresh observations I make in *The Best Laid Plans*.

Ruth Johnson, chief psychiatric social worker in the Psychiatric Department, with a wisdom enriched by years of work as a psychotherapist, provided many thoughtful observations both as a consultant and an interviewer for the project. Norman Jacobson, professor of political theory, a teacher in the Experimental College Program and therapist in the Psychiatric Department, as an interviewer and a consultant for the project, often provided a broad frame of reference for my thinking and, by his gift for analogy, metaphor, and speculation provided an opportunity for me to increase my insight into the processes of change. My friends Mervin Freedman, Steve Rauch, and Robert Roller all gave a sophisticated helping hand with the interviewing in the early phases of the project.

Aside from those who participated directly in the research, I owe a special debt of gratitude to the students who so generously shared their experiences with us; to Ellen Wilde, secretary to the Experimental College Program, who contributed important observations to the study; and to the faculty of the program for their participation as subjects and informants. I am particularly grateful to Joseph Tussman for making the research possible, not simply for his willingness to have the program observed but especially for his patience in having the research intrude upon his professional life.

I wish to thank Joseph Katz (then project director, Student Development Study, Human Problems Institute, Stanford University) for making available the personality scale scores from his study of the Berkeley students who graduated in 1965. We used these scores for the comparisons described in Chapter Seven. Such generous exchange of data can facilitate studies that otherwise would be too difficult and costly to carry out. I also wish to thank Professor Samuel Schaaf, College of Engineering, University of California, Berkeley, for allowing me to use the material that appears in Chapter Nine. Because of his interest as a member of the faculty of the Experimental College Program, he compiled and analyzed the records of performance of students in our study during their second two years in college.

Institutions also were important to the study: the Student Health Service housed us for five years and provided financing during the first year; the Office of Education, Bureau of Research, Department of Health, Education and Welfare, supported us financially by means of a contract during the last four years (Project No. 6-1293; Contract No. DEC-4-7-061293-1577).

As to writing a book, I find it very much like working with someone in psychotherapy or teaching a class: when the work is complete it becomes clear how it might have been done better. I have been sustained in the effort by the interest of a number of friends, some of whom are working in related areas: Harriet Renaud, Mervin Freedman, Jerry Gaff, Paul Heist, and Harvey Peskin. My friends Emma Marie Bartelme and Bill Robinson, and my wife, Barbara, read parts of the manuscript and made comments and suggestions that were helpful to my thinking.

Finally, it is appropriate to note that Chapter Three and Chapter Seven are based on material previously published. Chapter Three is an expansion of an article by the same title which appeared under my name in the *Journal of Higher Education,* 1970, *41* (8). The basic material in Chapter Seven was presented by Elizabeth Alfert and me in an article in the *Journal of Higher Education,* 1971, *42* (1).

The Best Laid Plans is dedicated to Barbara, Christopher, Peter, Thomas, and William.

Berkeley, California   ROBERT F. SUCZEK
September 1972

Contents

The Best
Laid Plans

*A Study of Student Development
in an Experimental College Program*

Chapter 1

Chronicle of a Research Project

*T*he start of the Experimental College Program (ECP) in 1965 occasioned the initiation of our study. It is assumed, that students will change during their college years, in part because of the educational experience. This assumption provided an opportunity to determine the factors that influence the nature of change—how changes in students in the Experimental College Program might contrast with those of students in the regular lower division program. Thus change is the central theme of the study. In general the study focuses on the development of young men and women in late adolescence during their college years. The particular emphasis is on the changes that take place in students who are in learning situations that differ in the kind and amount of

1

structure and in the interaction possible between students and teachers. The first interest defined by myself and Elizabeth Alfert, the psychologists who were the basic research team, was whether young men and women make use of such different educational situations to enhance their development in some way. Do they show greater or more varied development in one or another of these educational situations?

We were also interested in learning about the ways in which young people develop while they are students in college. Our interest included those students who do not appear to change at all and those who make a change that seems to contribute little to their development. We were also intent on learning more about what interests young men and women in college as well as about the pathways they take in pursuit of those interests, including the path that leads away from college before the completion of work for a degree. My previous work had stimulated a special interest in the college dropout (Suczek and Alfert, 1965).

In the course of the study we found ourselves changing our ideas not only about students, teachers, and the educational structure, but also about psychological research. In the last year of the study we changed our primary question and method of observation; we discovered that changes in attitudes and values in our culture were changing the nature of the very process we were studying. No doubt these value changes began well before our study was initiated, but we had not perceived them at that time. Change was becoming virtually an ideology. The process of change we were studying—a process which in the past had been taken for granted by those undergoing it as a natural and essentially inevitable experience and which only occasionally was consciously considered—became a conscious concern and was an experience deliberately sought by students. Change itself had taken on a positive value.

During the spring and summer of 1965, discussion of the shortcomings of higher education was accelerating. Many proposals for change were made. One of the qualities most frequently deplored was the machinelike aspect of undergraduate education, especially in the lower division, which purportedly ground up succeeding generations of freshmen into unthinking but well-trained cogs to fit the needs of our contemporary technological society.

Other qualities under attack were irrelevance of course study material in the face of contemporary social problems and the lack of opportunity for the student to pursue his own academic interests. These factors were believed compounded by the impersonality of large classes and a general lack of professional interest: in students as students, in students as individuals, and in the teaching process itself. This oversimplified, overstated perception was vocally and stridently stated by activists, and if it was not shared, at least it was given official recognition by many students and by many members of the faculty. It was epitomized in a speech by Savio (1964) to a Free Speech Movement rally: "There is a time when the operation of the machine becomes so odious, makes you so sick at heart, that you can't take part, you can't even tacitly take part, and you've got to put your bodies upon the gears and upon the wheels, upon the levers, upon all the apparatus, and you've got to make it stop. And you've got to indicate to the people who run it, to the people who own it, that unless you're free, the machines will be prevented from working at all."

The proposal for an Experimental College Program which Joseph Tussman, who was then chairman, Department of Philosophy, University of California, Berkeley, had been developing would we hoped make possible, in a large public institution, a kind of engagement among students, teachers, and subject matter that usually is found only in small private schools. The program permitted a high degree of collaboration among a student, his teachers, and fellow students; he could work with large units or areas of knowledge—defined and integrated primarily by their meaning and not divided arbitrarily by administrative necessity; stimulated by the subject matter he could have an opportunity to develop his *own* interests; he could integrate and elaborate such interests both by himself and together with other students and faculty in small formal and informal groups. Evaluation of the student's progress was based on his current work; it was on an individual basis and consisted of written and oral criticism and discussion.

Such an educational milieu afforded experiences for a student far different from those usually encountered on a large college campus. Aside from the obvious value of the program as an integrative approach to learning and intellectual development, it was likely to provide students with different alternatives for personal development.

In part, then, our general question emerged from a prevailing atmosphere, critical of higher education; it was focused by the initiation of the Experimental College Program. We set out to investigate the developmental changes that students undergo and how they might differ in the experimental atmosphere as compared with that in the regular lower division program.

In part, our general question was a continuation of previous work. Earlier study of development during late adolescent college years was sparse until the Mellon Foundation studies carried out at Vassar during the early and middle 1950s. Sanford (1962a) describes the developmental pattern which those studies elucidated.

We were able to show that, on the average, the four years of college were marked by steady increases in imaginativeness and sensitivity, independence and sophistication of judgment, capacity to express in constructive ways our most human dispositions. Similarly, there were decreases in prejudice, narrow-mindedness, and stereotyped thinking. . . . But there were large individual differences, among colleges and among the students in a given college. Some students showed marked developmental changes, some little, and some seemed even to go backwards.

In beginning this study, we hoped to learn about one other way of doing things and what difference it might make in the process of development. Because the study concerned different educational structures, many psychologists might have seen it as an opportunity to study learning, especially in its cognitive aspects. Our interests however were in the development of the whole person. We were inclined to ask, "To whom and to what is the student attending, what is he thinking and feeling, and what does he do about it?"

Our theoretical background was in a dynamic psychology that recognizes development as a multidimensional process in which biological patterning, societal patterning, and self-patterning of experience and actions are of equal relevance. This concept emphasizes the primal importance of an individual's earliest encounters with his growing, changing body, with the social world, and with his emerging self. In these encounters the patterns of selection of response by the infant and child become increasingly directive in the molding of his development—a process that Frank (1966) aptly terms "learning to learn."

Our concept also recognizes the factor of periodicity in the process of development, successive periods being characterized by different and successively difficult developmental tasks (Erikson, 1950). These tasks emerge from biological growth (which requires new ways of functioning), from the demands and seductions of the socialization process, and from the evolving self-structure, a development which from early in childhood gradually comes to make its own demands on the individual. Thus, the challenges presented to the individual by these developmental tasks in their demands for new modes of behavior and their overall integration are central aspects of the developmental process.

We consequently regard the student's development at the time he comes to college to be a crucial factor in his further development during that period. Several of our questions focused on this point. Would the Experimental College Program be selective; that is, would it attract a particular type of student or one at a particular stage or level of development? How might the student's developmental state interact with the particular milieu he encountered in college? To what extent would the nature of his development make it possible for him to make use of his educational program in the pursuit of further development? What might be experienced as a challenge, and how would the student choose to cope with it?

A number of factors led to an attempt at the systematic study of these questions. Notable among prior studies of educational experiments are Meiklejohn's (1932) experiment at Wisconsin—an inspiration for the present experimental program—and the Bennington study (Newcomb, 1943). Although some measures were used to evaluate the Bennington students, no comparison was made with students in other educational settings. Our opportunity to study students in two different educational atmospheres at the same university readily suggested a systematic comparison as part of the research design.

Furthermore, our study followed on the heels of a large-scale study at Stanford University and at the University of California, Berkeley, in which some of us had participated (Katz and associates, 1968). That study, an intensive, longitudinal observation of student development, consolidated and extended much of the original work in this area by the Mellon Foundation studies at Vassar by following the progress of students through four undergraduate years at the two universities. The developmental status of the entire freshman class was evaluated by means of personality scales and again by the same scales at the end of the senior year. The students also responded to a detailed personal history questionnaire at the end of the fourth year. Intensive interviews were carried out each semester with selected samples of the young men and women being studied.

A similar method was used for our study. Observations during the previous study suggested that the major developmental shifts occur during the first years of college. We therefore chose to use personality scales at the time of entrance and at the end of the second year (which coincided with the end of the Experimental College Program), as well as at the end of the fourth year of college. We used Katz's scales, thereby intending to facilitate comparison of our respective groups of students without comparing the measures. (See appendix A for details of the measures used.) This proved to be a fortunate decision because these comparisons led to one of the most important observations of our study—namely, that the character of succeeding freshman classes was changing rapidly. We came to recognize that the effect of cultural change on our students was as important as the effect of their immediate personal experiences in college (see Chapter Seven and Chapter Ten). Thus, we first intended to compare individual development in two educational settings by means of personality scales. These personality scales were intended to provide quantitative scores reflecting the level of development students had achieved at the beginning, middle, and end of their college experience. In addition, we wished to learn about the process of development more directly by means of interviews. We planned to carry out this part of our method in a systematic way by interviewing certain students at regular intervals, once each semester. The first interviews followed a schedule stating general areas to be covered and some specific questions to be asked. We intended to learn about all aspects of the student's relationship to college, to his family, and to himself. Our questions were based on our knowledge of students from participating in the prior study, on our theoretical speculation as to what we felt should be important in the student's experience, and, perhaps dimly, our own remembered experiences as students. In essence, we asked our students what we thought was important, and at the end of our schedule we gave them a chance to talk about what they thought was important.

In spite of the imposition of this kind of interview structure, each student's individuality became apparent. After the second interview, we began to be able to identify them in terms of some of their prevailing qualities. For instance, David, in all of his social relations, seemed always to insist on failing and being rescued. Marian became known for her simple platitudes for every situation. Dan was determined from the start, that nothing at the university was going to interfere with the pursuit of his academic goals. We were especially attentive to the particular developmental task with which a student appeared to be dealing, and that task and his way of dealing with it gave him the quality we came to identify with him. To make way for this emerging individuality, we changed our interviewing style radically at this point. Although we carefully reviewed our knowledge and observations of college life and of the particular student we were about to interview and although we formulated what we thought were important questions, we kept our questions in the back of our minds and deliberately refrained from asking them. Instead, we encouraged the student to talk about whatever was interesting him at that time. Meanwhile, rather than attempting not to influence the interview, we often deliberately tried to do so. By stating our own views on the matter under discussion, we could observe how our student might react to a different point of view, to an observation about himself which he had not previously considered, or simply to an interested individual of a different generation.

As we introduced this change in our interviewing techniques, questions tended to emerge from the interviews themselves. Such questions elicited new information and impressions and tested our assumptions about the student as an individual.

In addition to interviewing, one member of our research group acted as participant observer in the Experimental College

Program. He was Harvey Powelson, director of the Department of Psychiatry in the Student Health Service on the Berkeley campus. Because of this identity, he became known to some as the Program shrink, although in no way did he function as such. The reason for his presence in the Program was known to the faculty and was stated explicitly to the students: as a psychotherapist he was interested in the process of learning and change and wished to observe the process in a different kind of change institution—an educational setting—than the one in which he usually worked.

In pursuit of his interests, Harvey sat in on faculty meetings and came to weekly meetings of the program personnel, as well as to occasional evening activities. He attended seminars of individual teachers over periods of time to observe continuing themes and patterns in the various processes and interactions. He attended different seminars to get impressions of teacher and student styles. He also spent time informally at the building that housed the Program. He engaged in spontaneous conversation with students or faculty in the commons room or elsewhere in the house. During the first year, these activities involved an average of at least a full day's time each week, and during the second year, less than a day. His observations were dictated on tape and transcribed for the research files. After the first few months, this method was modified in order to increase the time allowed for observation. His observations were discussed and recorded as part of the material emerging from a weekly staff conference about the research.

In that conference the observations of the participant observer assumed a place of importance. Gathered in a different way and in a different setting, they presented an enlightening contrast with observations of the same student made during an interview. To one of us interviewing, a student might appear to have certain qualities, but they were only vaguely or dimly suggested by what we learned during the interview. The juxtaposition of the interviewer's observations with some of those made by the participant observer often threw light on such subtle hints, sometimes confirming them, sometimes contradicting them, and they allowed us to develop an understanding of a student with some confidence.

The mutual enhancing of observations was sometimes reversed, and we found ourselves trying to understand incompatible observations. On one occasion, when we were considering observations (made available to us by chance) from three different sources, we were convinced we were talking about three different young women. Such experiences, although making us long briefly for the simplicity of one source of data, kept us acutely aware of the complexity of the problem of understanding the experiences and the development of an individual.

We were so impressed with these experiences comparing observations that we made every effort to maximize the number of sources of data open to us. We interviewed most of the teaching assistants who participated during the first year of the Program and all of the faculty. We asked them about their experiences with, and impressions of, individual students, especially those they felt had benefited or had been adversely affected in their development while in the Program. Fortunately, one member of the faculty who taught in the ECP during the first year (Professor Norman Jacobson, Department of Political Science, University of California, Berkeley) came to the Student Health Service as research political scientist immediately after he completed his teaching appointment in the program. Norman's interests were similar to those of our participant observer, and since his experience was in teaching, he came to the Psychiatric Department to investigate how learning takes place in a therapeutic situation. He participated in our staff discussions, where his observations of students who had been in his seminars in the ECP gave additional dimensions to our view of many of them.

The secretary of the ECP also proved to be an excellent participant observer. Ellen Wilde was a young woman with a Master of Arts degree in political science. She had a keen interest in this experiment in education. Ellen was the only person among all the staff and students who was in the building almost continuously from early morning to late afternoon, five days a week. She thus had the advantage of being able to observe the pattern of activity in the house. Her continual presence, as well as her natural interest in people, led to a fairly intimate acquaintance with many of the students and several of the faculty. All were inclined to air their troubles in her office and to seek her counsel, so she often had a privileged view of two sides of some of the issues and of the relationships that emerged. Although she had a great sense of privacy and made it a point never to reveal a personal confidence to the researchers, she did provide us with detailed observation of public occurrences in the building.

Another source of data was a two-page information questionnaire to which the students responded at the end of the second year and another, one page long, to which they responded at the end of the fourth year. The first asked for information about their families and their experiences on campus. We gathered such information about some of the students during the interviews, but we wished to know about all our students, including those whom we had not interviewed. Some of the questions reflected our expectations of what is important for development, based on our theoretical perspective—for example, family attitudes toward education and religion. Other questions were based on what we learned about a student's experiences in college thus far.

The second questionnaire, answered at the end of the fourth year, also was based in part on our categories and in part on theirs. It asked the students to summarize certain aspects of their college experiences by year: their living arrangements (including sex of partners), financial arrangements, leisure activities, primary academic interests, and experiences—either especially engaging or discouraging—in their academic work. Inquiry into their plans for the period immediately following graduation completed the questionnaire.

Other indirect sources of data for which we were not prepared but which became available to us during the course of the study were the Intellectual Autobiography written by the students at the end of the ECP, the registrar's records, and the records of the Student Health Service.

So, the three sources of our data were to be the personality scales, participant observation, and the two questionnaires. With the data from the personality scales we expected to be able to answer questions regarding differences in developmental change that might prevail for students in the two educational atmospheres. We felt the data from the interviews and other forms of participant observation would provide us with a way of understanding the nature of the two atmospheres as students experienced them. Our knowledge of individual students—from the participant observations as well as the questionnaires and interviews—would give us insight into the nature of the developmental changes they experienced.

We proceeded with this design and these methods of data collection. By the beginning of the fourth and final year, we completed much of the quantitative evaluation of the personality measures and developed answers to most of our original questions. We also found that our thinking, which had been the basis for asking those questions, underwent change. First, we could no longer consider each of the two educational atmospheres as sufficiently unitary, that is, internally consistent, to have the same measures applied. Individual students were having very different experiences in each atmosphere. The original concept of two different but comparable conditions now seemed too simple. Second, use of the scales was limited by ideological changes that took place before and during the period of the study. Student responses to our measures were, to a large extent, in terms of contemporary ideology rather than their own personality dispositions (see Chapter Ten). Furthermore, we now had the impression that change does not take place in linear form, as the before-and-after measure of our original design optimistically assumed. Finally, we doubted increasingly that change could be related to educational structure at all; there are too many other events in a student's life, including changes in cultural values, which, at least to some, made the process of change emerge as an ideal.

Thus, as the end of the study drew near, our original questions and some of the means of getting answers to them seemed anachronistic and inappropriate. We were forced to the conclusion that instead of continuing with the framework posing the university versus the Experimental College Program, it would be more appropriate to learn about the different developmental changes that students experience in college and the personal experiences to which those changes seem to relate. Instead of making the planned assessment by means of repeating the administration of the personality scales with which we began, we engaged the students in a spontaneous self-assessment. All the students were asked to come in to discuss the study with us (see Chapter Eight). These small group discussions, held at the end of the fourth year, produced some of our most interesting insights into students' experiences and the process of change (see Chapters Nine and Ten).

In summary, we began with an effort to study systematically the development of young men and women in different educational atmospheres. But by the time we obtained answers to our main questions, we discovered we had a new question, namely, whether it is possible, after all, to measure change and that to which it relates. In turning to a naturalistic form of inquiry in the last phase of the study, we set aside the question of the generality of the changes observed. We decided that we wished to learn about the nature and variety of individual change.

All first-semester freshmen accepted by the University of California, Berkeley, for the fall semester, 1965, were sent a letter during the summer by the dean of the College of Letters and Science. In the letter he described the Experimental College Program and invited those who were interested in it to apply. Applications were received from 285 students and from among these, 150 students—seventy-three men and seventy-seven women—were selected at random by the faculty of the ECP to participate in the program. The only criterion was that the student already must have satisfied the Subject A requirement, which meant that he would not have to take a noncredit course in English composition during the first semester. (During the period of the study, approximately 40 per cent of all entering freshmen were required to do so.)

We contacted these 150 students when they came to the Student Health Service for the physical examination required of all entering students. We introduced ourselves as psychologists doing research with the Student Health Service; we explained we were interested in learning what the people who come to college are like and what happens to them during the time they are there; and we asked each student whether he or she would be willing to participate in our study by responding to an attitude and opinion questionnaire sometime during the week. We did not add further details unless the student asked for them. All but five of the 150 students were interested in the study and made arrangements to respond to our questionnaire.

These 145 students in the Experimental College Program formed the first of three groups. The second group was a first comparison group and consisted of the 135 students who applied to the Experimental College Program but were not chosen by the random selection. These students were enrolled in the regular lower division program. They also were contacted at the time of their entrance physical examination, and all agreed to participate in the study.

A third group, providing a second comparison group, was made up of 209 freshmen who indicated they were not interested in the Experimental College Program, who had satisfied the Subject A requirement, and who were willing to participate in our study. Except for the latter two criteria, these students were randomly selected. They, too, were enrolled in the regular lower division program.

During the week prior to beginning of classes in September, the entire sample of 489 students responded to our personality questionnaire: the Attitude and Opinion Survey. Subsequently, a sample of thirty students (fifteen men and fifteen women) was selected at random from each of the three groups, a total of ninety. These students were asked by letter to participate intensively in the study by coming to a one-hour interview twice each academic year. All of them agreed to do so. After the first interview, a few students decided not to continue. Others who had agreed to come in for interviews dropped out of the ECP, and some dropped out of school altogether. All of these were replaced in our interview sample by students from the same group who had similar scores on the personality scales.

At the end of the second year, when the Experimental College Program drew to a close, students in all three groups were asked to respond once again to the Attitude and Opinion Survey and to the two-page questionnaire of factual information about themselves and their families. Of the original 489 students, 343 were still on hand and willing and able to respond.

At the end of the fourth year all students who had originally responded to our questionnaire and who were still on campus or living in Berkeley were telephoned and invited to participate in the group discussions. Two hundred sixty-five came to the discussions and answered our second information questionnaire. Early graduation, dropout, transfer, and illness account for the balance of our sample. Only six students were not interested in participation in our discussions.

The spirit with which students entered into the research was surprising and gratifying. Remarkably few did not wish to participate when we first approached them. Even so, they were willing to talk to us, enabling us to get some impressions of their feelings and reasons for refusal. Their primary concern was a fear of violation of their privacy as a result of responding to our questionnaire. Some blamed their concern on their parents. Some who wished to stop after the first interview also did so because they wished to protect their privacy. Others simply offered practical reasons for not continuing, primarily lack of time. A few students felt that the project was not important enough to take up their time. They agreed with the ultimate intention of our research—to improve higher education—but they did not agree with our procedure.

However, the majority of those we asked did agree to participate and did so with a spirit of engagement and cooperation. They certainly felt free to complain and to offer suggestions. They appeared to enjoy contributing to research even if they did not gain directly from it themselves. This view of our study forecast an attitude which we later found to be prevalent among our students: in anything they undertake an important consideration is whether it is contributing to the community well-being.

By the time they were seniors, these young men and women were much more interested in being active participants in the study rather than passive subjects answering questionnaires. They responded eagerly to the idea of a group discussion of their impressions of our observations. A considerable number demurred at the idea of accepting monetary reimbursement for their time. (We paid them anyway.)

The students who came in for interviews expressed the most positive feelings about their contacts with us. Several told us it was the only experience of its kind that they had in college. It gave them, they said, an opportunity to review what they were thinking and doing and to gain perspective on themselves. Some told us they felt it was the only time that someone on campus took an interest in what they thought and what they were doing.

By the time of the final group meetings, the students were

keenly interested in the study, inquiring about the findings, making criticisms of the methodology, and requesting to be notified of the publications. Since they knew we did not intend to identify individuals in our writing, we took this to be a mark of their interest in the educational experiment itself.

Initially, we assured the students that participation was voluntary and that personal information would be confidential to the researchers. We had no hidden agenda or strategy in any part of what we asked them to do. They were informed of our research aims from the outset. We did not, however, emphasize our interest in change and development because we feared that, in their inclination to please, the students might stress unduly that aspect of their lives. Some did anyway.

One ethical consideration arose from the coincidence of some of our professional activities. Several of us working on the study were also working as psychotherapists in the Psychiatric Department of the Student Health Service. Inevitably, some students we met as patients later were encountered during discussion in the research conference. It was difficult to refrain from combining the observations from the two sources. After due consideration, in fact, we decided to combine the two, and we found it beneficial to a clear understanding of the student in both the clinical and the research perspective.

Our observations are much more elaborate and detailed and our knowledge of the educational atmosphere is much more thorough for students in the ECP than for those in the regular program because our basic work force was severely limited. It consisted of a project director (the author) and the assistant research psychologist, Elizabeth Alfert. Neither worked over half time on the project and often less than that. The other three participants in the work (Harvey Powelson, Norman Jacobson, and Ruth Johnson, chief psychiatric social worker of the Psychiatric Department, Student Health Service, University of California, Berkeley) contributed by interviewing students and by meeting with some of the discussion groups. During the last year and a half, they formed the balance of the weekly staff conference. Our observations of the regular undergraduate program were limited to what we could learn from the students we interviewed from that program. We did not have the manpower to observe them directly.

As the study progressed we became increasingly aware of the discrepancy between the systematic measures and what we knew of individual students. The measures led to speculative understanding heavy with abstractions, whereas personal contacts led us to believe we were dealing with a very different person than one suggested by our abstractions. Too often we found we could not reconcile the two. In this report I deal with them separately. Chapters Three, Five, Six, and Seven present findings about group change based on the quantitative measures, and Chapters Nine and Ten present findings about individual change based on our observations.

A final word about participation in the collection and analysis of the data: I describe this first trial of the Experimental College Program from my own image of it—an image that emerged from my interaction with the people and the events that took place during the four years of the study. I am aware that others have different views. I am reasonably certain that my view differs in various respects from Tussman's and that it does not represent his ideal of the program (that presented in Chapter Two), nor does it describe his subsequent effort to carry out the idea of the program with a new group of students and faculty.

In the same vein, the results in the form of generalizations— the generalized image of the students emerging from the quantitative aspects of the study—are constructions based on a statistical analysis of the measures. The images of the faculty and of individual students also are constructions emerging from our observations and from my personal experiences with those people.

One observation that is particularly clear in my mind as a result of this study is that each one of us has his own construction of the world. Individuality, not generality, of experience is the theme emerging most often for me from the experiences in this study.

The chapters that follow are arranged in a sequence that roughly follows our process of observing and learning about the students during four years. We appear personally in some of them because as participant observers we entered into the process, affected it, and were, in turn, affected by it.

Chapter 2

Perspective of the Experimental College Program

*T*he Experimental College Program was more than another curricular innovation. It was a statement of the need to revitalize the lower division of the university, and as such it was a reassertion of a basic but neglected function of liberal education. This is the view held by Tussman, and it was as a corrective to what he perceived as a serious functional imbalance in the educational structure that he designed and instituted the experimental program at Berkeley.

Historically, education at the university level has been dedi-

cated to achieving a double goal: breadth of knowledge and understanding—ideally intended to equip the student to participate
rationally and responsibly in the social world—and the fine specialization required for the practical pursuit of career objectives.

In the university, fostering the development of specialized
knowledge tends to conflict with the cultivation of human understanding, a function traditionally identified with the college. In
ideal educational practice the distinction in function is maintained
with an equal emphasis on each: "the university for multiplicity and
knowledge; the college for unity and understanding" (Tussman,
1969, p. xiv). However, the emphasis now is more and more on the
former function, and interest in the importance of broad and unified
understanding has steadily diminished. Specialized programs in
graduate school increasingly have first call on resources and teaching
energies in the university. Specialization in graduate school in turn
defines the function of the upper division as a preparation for
specialization. The resources of the university and, especially, the
teaching interests of the faculty are devoted primarily to these two
levels. The lower division, in the opinion of Tussman, is neglected.
Here, the fundamental purpose of the college must be strongly re-
asserted: "for the sake of all of us, for society and for the individual,
[that purpose is] to develop our rational powers, to heighten sensitivity to and awareness of fundamental human problems, to culti-
vate and strengthen the habits and dispositions which make it possible for humanity to displace the varieties of warfare with the institutions, the practices, and the spirit of reasoning together." In
short, the purpose of the college is "to fit us for the life of active
membership in the democratic community; to fit us to serve, in its
broadest sense, our common political vocation" (pp. 3–4). Such a
purpose requires an educational program equally as well planned,
integrated, and supported by the interests of the faculty as are those
in the areas of specialization. The miscellaneous collection of courses
extant in the lower division, largely unrelated and unintegrated,
does not constitute a program at all, let alone a program designed
to achieve such lofty purposes.

To correct this deficiency, Tussman proposed a first program, coinciding with the first two years of college, to be carried out
in the lower division of the University of California College of

Letters and Science. A first program should have several important characteristics. It should have exclusive, or nearly exclusive, call on the attention and energies of the student. The student must have ample time to do his work: to read, to think, to read again if he is so moved, and, finally, to write, after due and comfortable time for reflection rather than with the haste and urgency attendant upon a deadline. The program must be structured to enable close collaboration between student and teacher so that the teaching can be closely coordinated with the learning; in areas where the student's functioning needs development, such development can be fostered over time and in relation to different work. Finally, and perhaps most fundamental, the program must have an integrated and coherent curriculum that engages the student in thinking about basic problems of a democratic society and of a citizen in such a society.

In 1965 the regular lower division program at Berkeley apparently had none of these qualities. If present at all, they were in greatly attenuated form in an occasional course or tutorial and essentially were invisible. The regular program, to which the Experimental College Program stands in contrast, is the aggregate of courses offered students in the first two years in the lower division of the College of Letters and Science. There is no program in the sense of a planned or coherent organization of courses. Each department offers a large number of courses for the beginning student. There are many departments, and each has its particular requirements in addition to those of the College of Letters and Sciences. Requirements of a general sort are intended to develop skill in foreign languages and in writing one's own language; prerequisites give background for later specific majors; and some courses give a broad overview of a particular academic field. All these courses are taught in the many departments by a variety of teachers with various interests in teaching. Thus, no program in the sense of either thematic organization or purpose unifies or relates these courses to each other, nor is there unity in the sense of communication among the teachers concerning a common interest in teaching lower division courses.

This academic arrangement poses certain challenging problems for the teacher, and his efforts to resolve these problems in turn contribute some of the salient qualities of the academic atmosphere in the lower division. Tussman (pp. 6–7) describes the teachers' problems:

> *The course forces teaching into small, relatively self-contained units. Horizontally, courses are generally unrelated and competitive. That is, the student is taking three or four or even five courses simultaneously. They are normally in different subjects, given by different professors, and, with rare exceptions, there is no attempt at horizontal integration. Thus, each professor knows that he has a valid claim to only a small fraction of a student's time and attention. The effect is that no teacher is in a position to be responsible for, or effectively concerned with, the student's total educational situation. The student presents himself to the teacher in fragments, and not even the advising system can put him together again.*
>
> *What is worse is that the professor knows that even his fragment of the student's time must be competitively protected. If he does not make tangible, time-consuming demands the student diverts time to courses which do make such demands. It becomes almost impossible to set a reflective, contemplative, deliberate pace in a single course. The tendency is to overassign work, with the expectation that it will probably not all be done. The cumulative effect on the student is brutal. To survive he must learn how to not do his work; he is forced into the adoption of the strategies of studentship; he learns to read too fast, to write and speak with mere plausibility. His educational life, through no fault of his own, becomes a series of artificial crises.*
>
> *Horizontal competitiveness and fragmentation of student attention are limiting conditions of which every sensitive teacher is bitterly aware. But there is nothing he can do about it. He can develop a coherent course, but a collection of coherent courses may be simply an incoherent collection. For the student, to pursue one thread is to drop another. He seldom experiences the delight of sustained concentration. He lives the life of a distracted intellectual juggler.*

A student who is sophisticated and skilled in understanding and manipulating such a system may be able, if he wishes, to select a group of courses or teachers to achieve some coherence in his educational experience. Few freshmen have such talents. Tussman is firm in concluding that "the only effective educational unit for educational planning is the program" (p. 9).

The competitive horizontal pressures are removed. A single outside course (i.e., outside the program) can be accommodated without distraction (although more than a single course would probably destroy everything). Attention can be focused or concentrated, and decisions about simultaneous lines of activity can be made within the program on purely educational grounds. We can make possible exclusive attention to a single work for a sustained period. We can integrate or coordinate virtually the entire range of the student's academic activity—reading and writing, lecture and discussion. We can set our own pace and establish our own rhythm.

Vertically, continuity for a two-year period seems about right. While a single year is better than nothing, the second year brings to fruition and reinforces what the first year only begins. Two years is far more than merely twice as good as a single year. Such continuity provides ample opportunity to develop curricular themes and variations and to ensure variety and balance. It also makes possible a relaxed, confident, long-range approach to the development of particular skills and powers. We can, for example, think in terms of a sustained two-year program of writing. Development is discernible and can be fostered.

The program, unlike the course, is a workable educational unit. It presents us with the whole student for a significant period of time. It restores to the teacher a rather frightening share of responsibility for the student's education—a responsibility which seems to evaporate from the interstices of the course system. Educational decisions become necessary; more importantly, they become possible. The program recaptures for the teacher the possibility of giving a reasonable structure to the life of learning [p. 10].

The idea for this kind of program was stimulated by Tussman's association with Alexander Meiklejohn. Meiklejohn, an educator known for his ideas about liberal educational reform, was invited to the University of Wisconsin, where, in 1927, he developed an Experimental College Program, an integrated program of study for a group of lower division students. Tussman, subsequently a student of Meiklejohn's, had considered the idea of such a program for a long time. He discussed it with colleagues and with administrators in the chancellor's office and with the president. In the 1964–1965 academic year both colleagues and administrators were receptive to the idea, and it was possible to put it into specific form. The program began in the fall of 1965, simultaneously with the beginning of the period of questioning and reform in higher education which followed the explosive Free Speech Movement at Berkeley.

Preliminary planning defined the form of the Experimental College Program—a form determined in collaborative effort by the faculty during the spring and summer preceding the start of the program. The ideal version which Tussman and his colleagues hoped to achieve might be described as follows. (I have written it here in the form of a prospectus. There was then no time to prepare such a statement.)

This first program is intended for the entering freshman as a beginning and a foundation for his educational experience in college. It is not meant for any special student or to require special talents. The program attempts to enroll a full range of entering freshman students, the only exception being those who have not satisfied minimum standards for writing the English language. (At Berkeley such students must take a beginning English course during their freshman year. The time-consuming nature of the course would preclude their participation in the program.)

When a freshman is admitted to the program he is expected to commit himself for the entire two-year period. A student is not prevented from leaving if he so desires. His wish to do so, however, is discussed with him by the faculty, and a decision to stay or leave is based on careful consideration of his educational development. If it appears to be educationally to his advantage, he is encouraged to leave. Ideally, in many instances, because of the opportunity offered by the two-year period, the advantage is in staying in a situation where educational problems can be worked out with thoughtful consideration for the student's full development.

The advantages offered by the two-year period are further enhanced by the small size of the program, which is limited to 150 students. The faculty consists of six full-time teachers whose only professional responsibility is the program. The student-faculty ratio of twenty-five to one is the same as in the university. (Problems of recruiting faculty resulted in five faculty staffing the program in the first year, with five graduate student teaching assistants.) But the fact that the teachers have none of the usual demands on their time, such as research and committee work, makes it possible for them to maintain a careful, continuous consideration of the student's educational needs, development, and problems.

Just as the faculty can give full attention to the student, the student's full attention to the program also is made possible by this structure. It is his central educational experience for the two-year period. He is free to take one course each semester from among the regular lower division offerings and is encouraged to use that option to fulfill the university language requirements. Other than this one course, the program itself satisfies all academic requirements (for the student in liberal arts) so that, at the end of the second year, the student has the necessary credits to go directly into his junior year in the university.

Engagement in the educational process of the program is encouraged further by the fact that the program is separately housed. All activities are carried on in one building, which contains all faculty offices, a library-study room, meeting rooms for seminars, and a commons room, where the faculty and students can assemble. An air of informality is encouraged, and students are free to use the building both as a center for their formal intellectual activities and as a hangout where informal pursuit of social and esthetic interests may continue.

The absence of many of the usual academic bureaucratic routines also helps to provide an atmosphere of informality and freedom from pressure. There is time to be engaged fully in the program. Regular lectures are not the primary instructional method. There are no quizzes, no exams, and no grades. The readings that form the basic material of the curriculum are assigned so that there is ample time to read them more than once. Meanwhile, the readings and the ideas they stimulate are discussed in a small, twice-weekly seminar. Occasionally, if it is appropriate, a lecture amplifying some aspect of the matter being studied is given by one of the faculty or a guest who brings special knowledge or sophistication. Ample time also is available for writing the assigned papers. During the process, the teacher can be consulted easily. The thinking expressed in the student's papers is examined personally and fully by the teacher, either in writing or in discussion in regularly held tutorial meetings.

Such interaction encourages in the student a lively sense of himself, of his own thinking, writing, and intellectual process, not as he is judged against other students, but in terms of himself—where he is now in comparison to where he has been and where he is going in his intellectual development. Each term of study the student has a different member of the faculty acting as his seminar leader, tutorial teacher, advisor, and general mentor. During two years he has the opportunity to work intensively with six different teachers. The process of evaluation of his functioning is ongoing, however, providing a personal sense of continuity.

Continuity and coherence in the program also are provided by the curriculum. Although profound in its intentions, the curriculum is fairly simple in design. The purpose of the program is what the purpose of the lower division should be: "to fit us for the life of active membership in the democratic community; to fit us to serve, in its broadest sense, our common political vocation" (Tussman, 1969, p. 4). The program attempts to achieve this ambitious undertaking with a curriculum that consists of four periods in the history of Western man. These periods involved men in major crises that centered on issues and institutions which also are apparent in our democratic society today. To examine those crises in their original context is to examine analogues of dilemmas today. Thus, the curriculum of the program is indeed a "rich version of the basic moral curriculum of our culture" (p. 54). A list of the readings is in Appendix B.

The Greeks constitute for us a great exemplary episode. Its dramatic center is the Peloponnesian War seen through the eyes of Thucydides. But everything we read illuminates that tragedy. Homer is in the background; Aeschylus, Sophocles, Euripides are brooding commentators; Plato reaps its lesson. It is an unparalleled chorus for the basic human plot. We echo it in everything we do. It is the great introduction to ourselves. . . . The seventeenth century . . . happens to be where we pick up the other great cultural strand of our lives. It gives us the King James Bible, Shakespeare, Hobbes, and Milton—the Judeo-Christian tradition in a strain especially constitutive of the American tradition and character. As for America, we take the covenant, the Constitution, the law, and the court, the living complex institution, as the thread which guides us in the attempt to understand what we are up to. We have followed this thread haltingly but will persist with growing confidence. We are the people of the law if we are anything.

The fourth and final crisis considered is one of those through which we now are living, the racial revolution, to be studied by directly observing the community, its institutions, and current problems.

Similarities in institutions, problems, and conflicts dealt with in these four periods give the curriculum thematic continuity and relevance to the student's educational experience. The fact that it is a curriculum predetermined by the faculty (as compared with student-initiated curriculum or individual contract) also may provide a moral lesson in action for the potential citizen of a democracy: his freedom to function independently within the structure of the program is guaranteed by his own efforts to maintain the structure by carrying out his responsibilities to obey the rules and to the faculty developing the program.

Coherence in the program is achieved by having all students and faculty use a common set of readings simultaneously in the different seminars. For this reason, any student can talk with any member of the program—faculty or student—about what he is reading or writing and enjoy an informed response.

All the readings used to make up this basic moral curriculum of our culture are primary sources; they are writings from the period being studied and are regarded, for the most part, as classics or masterpieces. Although each book originated in a particular historical period, the themes and ideas it expresses are universal; "a classic escapes from or transcends its generative context" (p. 57). The readings, then, function as symbolic expressions of fundamental human themes concerning the contradictions of man seeking personal freedom within the social order. In this respect, also, the program curriculum achieves unity.

It follows that the faculty need not be expert in the periods studied or in any particular field. The program "requires of the teacher intelligence, the ability to read, and some understanding of the teaching process" (p. 60). The idea of an expert teaching what he is expert in is antithetical to the idea of the program.

Alternative periods and readings might have been used. These were chosen by the group who carried out the program as it is reported in this book. Others might have chosen differently. In fact, Tussman expected that others would come forward from the university community at the end of the two years and say, "I think I can do it better another way." (None did. See Chapter Eleven for a discussion of the problems of staffing programs such as these.) Had this occurred, these teachers would have become the faculty for the next two-year period.

A final consideration necessitates returning to the idea that a first program is specifically an education for effective participation in a democracy. In this connection, Tussman (p. 66) writes:

> *Democracy is an organized and complex state of life, and it requires the cultivation of its appropriate state of mind. That state of mind, which alone can sustain the institutions of democracy, does not develop naturally or by neglect. The democratic nature is also a "second nature," and it needs deliberate nurturing. To be committed to democracy is to give a special mandate and a special character to the school and college. Freedom is the fruit of the successful operation of the teaching power. Freedom is power, and it, too, must be deliberately cultivated. It rests on discipline, not whim; on habit, not impulse; on understanding, not desire. It is a difficult achievement.*

Had a prospectus for the program been written, it certainly would have included the above quotation as a statement of what the program is and what it stands for. After its first two-year trial, Tussman added a caution as to what the program was not: "The spirit of the program, however, with its completely required faculty-determined curriculum and structure is utterly alien to the spirit of 'student-initiated' programs, which involve students in the creation and planning of courses in which they are interested or which, in one way or another, turn them loose to educate themselves" (p. vii). In short, both the content and the structure were intended to emphasize the theme that freedom is achieved only within the framework of a delineated structure.

What the program was and was not to be was not as clearly articulated by the faculty doing the planning in the summer of 1965. In the first trial, as with any human enterprise, many of the problems anticipated never emerged, and many that were not anticipated did present themselves and absorbed much faculty energy. In many superficial, and in some fundamental respects, the program—in its first trial—differed from what it was intended to be. This difference was of particular interest to me since the human condition is inherently disjunctive, full of complexity, contradiction, and ambiguity. In spite of apparent agreement during preliminary planning, there were wide differences in how each faculty member conceived the program. At times this conflict of views produced such unexpected consequences that the experience must have had—especially for Tussman—the unreal quality of a nightmare. Even so, the program continued, the students participated in it, and the experience had important consequences for both students and faculty.

Chapter 3

Self-Selection and Special Educational Programs

"*I*t takes a crook to catch a crook," an age-old aphorism, suggests that a policeman has certain qualities that suit him for the job and implies a certain amount of self-selection for his job. Heist, McConnell, Matsler, and Williams (1961) demonstrate that it takes a special student to "catch" a special college; that a student with high intellectual interests finds a college that caters to such interests; and that such self-selection, in part, accounts for the unusual productivity of students who do exceptional work. Maslow shows that studies of unconventional behavior tend to interest volunteer subjects who particularly enjoy their own unconventionality (Maslow and Sakoda, 1952). Roe's studies (1953) tell us that self-selection produces a degree of similarity in personality characteristics in some professions. In another related area of study, Heist and Webster (1959) found that personality scores for groups in different academic majors differ significantly.

Colleges, majors, occupations, and so on are known entities with fairly well-defined bodies of myths, expectations, and images which individuals can perceive and which form the basis for their decision to enter into them. The importance of self-selection, in any case, is the fact that the people involved bring some uniform characteristics to the situation, and this factor helps make the college, the occupation, or the major what it is and tends to perpetuate it in that form. Similarly, an individual's characteristics also may be perpetuated because of their congruence with the situation; that is, he may not change or develop in other ways as a result of his experience in that college, major, or occupation.

The factor of self-selection is relevant in connection with the educational experiments and efforts at reform currently under way in our colleges and universities. Since the early part of the 1960s, experiments with revised curricula and teaching methods have been increasing, especially in undergraduate programs, where dissatisfaction with conventional programs has been particularly keen. In this contemporary upsurge of innovation and experiment, the question of self-selection is important in several respects. The nature of an experimental program depends, in large part, on the nature of the students who participate in it. Many experiments and innovations are being devised to provide options for students, thus offering increased possibilities for their intellectual and personal growth. Selection of the participants, if it results in a homogeneous grouping, may defeat the purpose of the experimental course or program. For example, a special course may intend to provide an experience of freedom in expression of ideas for students inhibited or inexperienced in such expression. If the students who participate lack inhibitions in expressing themselves, such a course may be not only useless but detrimental to the development of students who need experience in self-control.

Many contemporary experiments allow any student in good standing to participate. That is, in order to provide options for all students who want them, these courses and programs intentionally are not selective. In contrast to colleges, majors, and occupations, experimental courses are new and do not have enduring and well-defined characteristics. Nevertheless, do such courses involve a degree of self-selection large enough to influence their outcome? That is the question being considered.

This four-year study of the effects of the educational process on personality development provides an opportunity to make some observations about this question. Since the Experimental College Program was new, developed largely during the summer immediately preceding its initiation, no well-developed image or mythology was associated with it. A few of the students who applied for it had seen Tussman on a television show dealing with educational reform and had some impression of what a program initiated by him might be like, but the large majority had nothing to go on except a brief description of the program, which was circulated to all entering freshmen in the letter from the dean.

In their responses to the Attitude and Opinion Survey during their first week on campus, students interested in the experimental program differed significantly ($p < .01$) in several characteristics from students not applying for the program (Table 1). Their scores suggest that, as a group, they were relatively more flexible, tolerant, and realistic in their thinking; they were less bound by authority as institutionalized in family, school, church, and state; and they were less dependent on authority, rules, and rituals for managing their social relationships. They tended to take a relatively strong position opposing authoritarian and ethnocentric attitudes.

They were freer to express their impulses than were other freshmen. They were impunitive in attitude but able to behave aggressively in a way appropriate to the situation; they were more interested in intellectual pursuits and had diverse interests, especially in artistic matters of all kinds; that is, they were esthetically oriented. They were less interested in science and quantitative problem solving and tended to earn significantly lower scores in mathematical achievement tests.

Table 1

DIFFERENCES IN PERSONALITY MEASURES OF FRESHMAN STUDENTS

Measure	Applying to ECP		Not Applying		t
	$\overline{X}$	S	$\overline{X}$	S	
Social Maturity	106.6	15.1	100.5	17.3	4.10**
Impulse Expression	66.7	16.6	63.2	18.7	2.15*
Schizoid Function	51.4	15.4	50.2	15.6	.80
Estheticism	34.9	8.1	31.4	9.0	4.46**
Developmental Status	46.7	9.9	42.4	11.6	3.45**
Masculinity-Femininity	44.5	8.2	48.6	10.3	4.82**
Ethnocentrism	33.5	10.7	37.8	12.1	4.20**
Authoritarianism	78.1	19.2	83.7	21.6	3.07**
Scholastic Aptitude Test					
Verbal	625.2	70.3	631.1	65.2	.83
Math	579.4	86.3	644.8	86.7	5.18**
Average	611.5	61.7	638.2	64.6	4.00**

*$p < .05$
**$p < .01$

NOTE: $\overline{X}$ is the arithmetical mean of scores for the group. S is the standard deviation of the mean score. t is the ratio between the two mean scores. p is the statistical significance of the ratio (that is, of the difference).

They were relatively more open. They more freely admitted problems of adjustment and feelings of anxiety and personal inadequacy, and they were more likely to seek satisfactions in social relationships.

In brief, the personality scale scores show systematic differences in attitudes and values. These differences suggest that the freshmen interested in this special educational venture were relatively more flexible and independent than were their peers; they had broader intellectual and esthetic interests; and they were personally more open, more expressive, and more aware of themselves.

Scores of students not volunteering for the program suggested a personality like that of the typical college freshman described by Sanford (1962b): conventional, compliant to authority, somewhat constricted, and inhibited. He (or she) is dominated by a strong conscience which is opposed to impulses and subjective feelings and favors a rational, task-oriented life. In his struggle to control impulses according to the demands of his conscience, his ego seemingly gains much support from the organization, the demands, and the authoritarian structure of a typical undergraduate program of required classes.

To put it another way, students choosing the conventional program more often perceived themselves as being most acceptable, most personally valued, and safest in the role of passive learner, looking up to and accepting the authority of the teacher on all matters. "What does he want me to know" is a perfect expression of this position, which makes for predictability in the world as the student sees it.

By comparison, students choosing the experimental program more often appeared to have had a less constricting conscience and an ego freer to attempt integrating conscience and impulse. Or, in other words, the student's sense of value derived from maintaining a more autonomous position in respect to authority and conventional institutions and from having a special interest in the subjective, hence his keen involvement in self and in artistic things of all kinds. This outlook makes for predictability in the world as he sees it.

Both the students choosing the ECP and those rejecting it apparently were responding to the qualifying expressions in the dean's letter describing the Program. These were, for example, "departs rather sharply from the traditional pattern of lower division work . . . the program [will be] flexible, the spirit informal . . . risks as well as rewards . . . problems . . . will call for imagination and flexibility." The images aroused by those expressions could appeal to one person and threaten another.

One other factor is important to consider in concluding that consistent self-selection was reflected in the personality differences in the two groups. The dean's letter made it clear that being in the program would present great difficulties to anyone planning to major in the physical sciences. Thus, the differences in personality characteristics possibly reflect exclusion of prospective physical science majors. To evaluate this hypothesis, students from both groups without plans to pursue a science major were compared in terms of the personality scales. Even accounting for the science factor, the scale differences between those interested in the ECP and those not interested are significant. In short, self-selection based on personality characteristics seems beyond question. Those students who were selected randomly for participation in the ECP had mean scores on our personality measures very similar to those who volunteered and were not selected. Essentially the same characteristics of self-selection may be inferred.

In a two-year educational program such as this one, the process of self-selection continues. By the end of the first semester seventeen students transferred out of the program. As a group, transfer students had significantly lower mean scores on two of our personality scales than did the students continuing in the program. They were less flexible, less tolerant of the unknown and the different, and had less interest in esthetic and intellectual pursuits. In interviews following their transfers they indicated they felt unable to work without more course structure or guidance.

A basic and general mechanism that makes sense of the phenomenon of self-selection is man's tendency to orient himself to the future. How the future is perceived determines whether the individual attempts to ensure his survival through change or through maintaining a status quo. During either the first or second interview in their freshman year, the students told us why they made the program choices they did. In many instances their reasons seemed casual. For example, a number of the students said that the program sounded "different," "exciting," or "an interesting thing to try." Some who felt this way also took into account the possibility that it would give them a background compatible with the major they were considering. In other words, they had nothing to lose. These examples, though indicating a casual attitude, suggest that an important element in their choice was their interest in the new and different and their willingness to take risks. The term *experimental* seems to have been enough to excite and interest many of them and to prompt them to apply.

Freedom from authority is a second theme of major importance in the student's perception of the Experimental College Program. Many instances indicate that students saw the program as a chance to be free to work independently: "a lot of independent time, and not structured"; "I hoped the freedom would provide a chance to learn how to organize my work myself." A very important component of the theme of freedom is the sense of specialness these students expressed about themselves and their ideas. It is clearly voiced by one student: "The Tussman Program is what I would have dreamed of. A chance to learn about literature and a chance to think and to create. It's *my* ideas which are important." A variation of this specialness is found in an identification with popular ideas about contemporary youth: "I saw Tussman on TV presenting his ideas in relation to alienated and unsatisfied students."

It is clear, from our observation and interviews, that many of these students regarded freedom and independence important not only as concepts but because freedom implies that their thinking can result in full, creative fruition: that under circumstances of freedom they will create was unquestioned by many. That they tended to be alienated and unsatisfied indicates lack of freedom. An occasional student, more clear and less romantic in his view of himself than the others, evaluated the freedom of the program more realistically: "My reasons for joining the Tussman college were not educationally meaningful ones. It sounded like a good thing to me to delay going through the hustle of the big U. The lack of pressure coupled with my lack of direction were a big part of the appeal."

One major view of the program by the students, then, was that it gave them freedom to express themselves creatively. But there was an opposite perception of the program. Some students did not apply because they perceived it as restricting: "I decided I didn't want to. It seemed a little limited, no language, no science. Also, you shut yourself off from the university for two years with 150 students"; "I wanted to experiment more with different courses"; "it sounded confining."

On the basis of the dean's letter, the content of the program was interpreted as follows: for some it was philosophy, others history, a study of literature, or the classics. One student said it sounded like "too poetic-artistic a life" for him.

So, for some students the future was "secured" by complying with their parents' wishes (a few entered the program expressly because of their parents' wishes). Some searched for the freedom they felt was necessary to function creatively, while others saw the freedom as providing a haven in which they would not have to make choices. We can infer that all these students were maintaining the status quo, each in his own way. Others apparently were seeking a change in themselves; they regarded the freedom as an opportunity to learn how to develop their own inner controls, their capacities to deal with ambiguous, unstructured, and many-faceted situations in the future.

Among those who chose the regular program there was also a division of opinion. The Experimental College Program attempted to offer an alternative to what was popularly regarded as a monolithic educational atmosphere. Some students saw the ECP as too free for them and chose instead the regular program, the tried and true, which they were accustomed to in their prior educational experiences. But others saw the new program as monolithic itself— narrow and confining, committing them to two years of work and associations they would have little or no choice about; these students chose the regular program for its freedom.

To return to the original theme, the Experimental College Program did catch, or was caught by, a special group of students. The individuals in the group varied considerably in many respects —for example, in their reasons for volunteering. Still, the degree of homogeneity was high enough in respect to certain attitudes to distinguish them from other students in the same freshman class.

The particular qualities of this group also are the qualities of the faculty, if one is to assume that faculty attitudes are reflected by the characteristics of the program. The program promised freedom from the usual constraints of lectures, examinations, and grades; freedom to experiment and to innovate; and high intellectual involvement.

Was this likely to be a good mixture? Were intellectual and personal development possible with this group of students and like-minded teachers? My general observation of groups gathered for purposes of interaction—therapy groups, intellectual discussion groups, conversation groups—suggests that a heterogeneous grouping involving some (not extreme) differences is likely to produce more interaction and hence more possibility of change than is a homogeneous group. Strauss takes a more extreme view than mine of the need for differences. "The possibility of alteration in anyone's range of vision is increased by intimate participation in groups composed of people as unlike oneself as possible. If one associates only with his counterparts there is less chance for radical conceptual change" (Strauss, 1969, pp. 29–30). Here however in the case of the Experimental College Program it is clear that in the homogeneous group there were vastly differing views of the program (and of the self) which made for different reasons for choosing the program and, implicitly, different kinds of interactions.

It will be necessary to study the development of individual students participating in the program to learn what kinds of interaction actually took place in such a mix of students and faculty and how the participants were affected. From the present observations it is clear that random selection from a population of volunteers does indeed produce a select group. Experimental classes and programs, in attempting to understand their success or their difficulties, must include in their considerations the factor of self-selection. In presenting a program to potential participants it might be important to take into account the needs of the students for whom the program is intended and to stress those qualities in the program that will appeal to that kind of student. Perhaps a description that includes qualities of a different, and even opposite, nature, so that a variety of choices is apparent, might be a way of counteracting extreme self-selection.

Of course, it is possible that the best all-round solution is a trial run. The students who left at the end of the first semester of the program may be thought to have wasted their time. Still, it was a very valuable experience (or could have been), because the students learned about themselves: they learned they could make a mistake and they could do something about it. There is no better lesson in judgment and self-reliance, both qualities considered ideal goals of a liberal education.

Chapter 4

Educational Atmospheres of the Two Programs

*I*n the early 1960s some short-comings and limitations in higher education, especially in large institutions, were being criticized. These shortcomings developed partly because the natural tendency of a bureaucratic organization is to compartmentalize and rigidify as it grows. In part the shortcomings were related to young people who felt that their rapidly changing needs were not well met by traditional programs and courses. Such criticism of higher education reached an acute stage about mid-decade and lent itself to a unitary perception of the "university." The popular image of the university was of a factory producing socially acceptable cogs for the industrial and business establishment. It was a uniform, uniformly applied and experienced system that tended to eliminate individuality and creativity and prevent the development of students except in narrow, technical, and skill-oriented directions. These criticisms were overstated; nevertheless, they reflected the atmosphere experienced by students, and, in turn, they represented an influence on the students' perception of their experiences.

Lack of coherence is important in the academic structure of the first two years at Berkeley (or, for that matter, at other large colleges of universities) and contributes substantially to the atmosphere. Although a student has a defined program, the courses vary in focus and breadth, in terms of providing background or developing skills. Even in the same department, the courses have little thematic organization or unifying purpose to enable a student to experience coherence in his program. Furthermore, the courses are taught by teachers with widely different styles and levels of interest.

Limitation of choice is another aspect of the lower division atmosphere. Various requirements must be met: a general development of skills as in language or mathematics; introductory courses presenting a broad view of a particular field of knowledge; prerequisites for later specialization. Choices more likely are available in terms of timing than of content. After a student locates himself in a particular subject area, he has little choice of courses to take, although he may decide when he will fulfill a particular requirement. It is not easy for a student to arrange a program coherently even if he has the sophistication to know how various parts are related. Lack of connection and lack of choice are heightened by specific demands for performance, especially since the demands are made without regard for those made by other courses. Quizzes, midterm and final examinations, and grades contribute to the general atmosphere a sense of schedules, pressure, and competition in what is known as the grade-point-average game.

Because Berkeley has a large enrollment, it produces an air of impersonality, most likely experienced in the lower division. A freshman student is new on campus and probably knows no one. He first experiences orientations and examinations (medical and academic) together with a large number of strangers. Unless he has an unusual program, many classes are large, some so large that his teacher uses a microphone. The possibilities of more than distant, cursory experiences with his teachers are limited by the large number of students, by the teachers' interests, and often by the student's unwillingness to acknowledge a wish to have a relationship with an adult. His contacts with officials of the college probably are official and impersonal. His most likely personal contact in the academic program is with a graduate student teaching assistant for a large course. Such contact does occur but not often.

For the most part, the students whom we studied who were not in the ECP had in the lower division relatively structured experiences in an academic setting that was segmented, characterized by conflicting demands, pressures, and impersonality. Competitiveness and isolation were important parts of their experience.

The Experimental College Program, begun when the monolithic image of the university was overemphasized in popular criticism, was regarded as the polar opposite of the university. The difference was emphasized because the ECP attempted to produce very different experiences for the students.

Besides eliminating arbitrary division of content into one-semester courses, the program eliminated other educational procedures growing out of bureaucratic needs which limit, hamper, or segment the educational process: routinely scheduled lectures as the primary mode of teaching, grades, and examinations. Perhaps these changes contributed primarily to the concept of the ECP as the opposite of the lower division program. The ECP achieved an image of total freedom, a place where students could do what they wanted and where they often were perceived as doing nothing by their peers in the regular program. Some did do nothing (but more of that later). Now I will detail some events so that the students' experiences in the ECP may be appreciated.

The program was housed in a separate building on the edge of campus. It was a large, three-story house, previously used by a fraternity and remodeled to accommodate faculty and staff offices, a library and study, a commons room, and several small seminar rooms. It was intended to be the center of all academic activities and also a place for informal social gatherings where students could hang out, talk, encounter each other and the faculty.

The faculty developed general plans to carry out the program, but specific month-by-month curriculum and activity planning were flexible, to be determined by the faculty as the program proceeded. The faculty members represented five disciplines. In addition to Tussman, who was chairman of the Department of Philosophy, it included one man from the Speech Department, acknowledged as a campus poet; one who had been chairman of the Aeronautical Sciences Department; one man from the Department of Political Science and a specialist in political theory; and from the Speech Department, one man who was a practicing attorney working exclusively with cases involving violations of individuals' civil liberties as guaranteed by the Bill of Rights. This faculty selected five graduate students—one woman and four men—as full-time teaching assistants. All these talented students were very interested in the educational experiment. A final important member of the staff was its full-time secretary, a young woman with an M.A. in political science and also an interest in this educational venture.

All eleven were talented and well-educated, different from each other, and, probably, each was certain of the rectitude of his position on many matters, although tolerant of different positions and opinions. It was not easy for the faculty, in their summer preliminary planning meetings, to agree on specific procedures except the general area of study for the first semester, a tentative schedule of weekly events, and the first readings. Since teachers are accustomed to working out their own plans and carrying them out in their own classrooms, in relative isolation from their colleagues, working together in the ECP was relatively a new experience and one that involved many difficulties. One of the greatest difficulties occurred when the faculty was likely to be most exposed to each other: the planned weekly assembly of the college at which faculty members were to speak. From the outset, these meetings—often abandoned and then reinstituted—were a major disappointment to faculty and students alike.

Some difficulties became manifest in the first weeks of the program. All students were asked to read Herodotus during the summer and come prepared to discuss him at the opening of the program. For almost two weeks after the opening of the fall semester, there was no discussion of Herodotus. There was no lecture at the weekly general meeting, as planned. At the general meeting during the first week there were a few announcements and a welcoming message to the students: "It's your house, your program." In the second week, again there was no lecture. In fact the faculty, although meeting together with the entire student body and assigning students to small seminar groups, was not much in evidence in the house during the first week or two. Apparently each one was, for his own reasons, reluctant or unable to begin. Since some teaching assistants made themselves available and apparently represented an approachable version of a teacher, the eager students flocked around them to discuss matters of interest to them—war, peace, death, God, sex, and drugs. During the first week as many as seventy-five to ninety students gathered in various groups and clusters in the house to talk to each other and some of the teaching assistants. Never again did that many come together spontaneously at one time in the subsequent two years of the program.

The fact that many students gathered around some of the teaching assistants did not make some of the faculty feel comfortable about their own distance from the students. Nor did it cement relationships with the teaching assistants, who were asked to try not to subvert the program by having "T groups" with the students.

In the third week it was agreed that, at the general meeting, each faculty member would make himself known by presenting his favorite passage from the Iliad and by discussing his reasons for choosing it. The program finally began. "Joe's College," as it came to be called, was under way.

As I indicated earlier, the idea of an experimental college grew in the imagination of Tussman as a result of his experiences as a student of Meiklejohn, who once conducted a similar experimental program. Early in 1964, after Tussman received a favorable response and promise of support from the president of the university, the idea was discussed by colleagues. A number of them became interested in an educational program that would be a collegial effort: several professors working together to develop a new curriculum and new ways of working with lower division students.

Although it would be an interruption of their regular academic advancement in their departments, the idea of working together prevailed. The interruption would last only two years. At the conclusion, another group might wish to conduct an experimental program of its own.

As the faculty members began working together intensively during the summer months preceding the beginning of the program, ideas for the curriculum were blocked out, possible readings were discussed, and ideas for meetings with students were considered. The group worked in concert to make it a collegial effort. No one acted as chairman or director. There was even an effort to lean backward to avoid putting anyone in that position. At times individuals gainsaid their own opinions to avoid dominating the group. All participated in the decisions—planning the program, selecting the teaching assistants, choosing the house and planning for refurbishing the house on a limited budget.

The house chosen was in poor condition, and many decisions had to be made concerning repairs and decoration. When repairs began and work and material orders had to be signed, one person was needed to do the signing. Tussman agreed to be that person. A host of housekeeping decisions also had to be made, often involving minute and trivial matters. To spare the time of the entire group for important considerations, it was agreed that Tussman should make these decisions also. The five-man faculty continued to work together. As the program advanced through the year, problems that arose were considered by the group, and group decisions were attempted. Some problems seemed refractory to a consensus. Under the usual arrangements in an academic department or committee, these would be decided by the chairman or by vote. Tussman, even though pressed by having to take the lead in other matters—and perhaps also because of being put in the leadership role—demurred from making decisions, even when urged to do so. Often, instead of being settled, these issues occasioned a drift. Repeated discussions brought no resolution of differences, so matters remained unsettled. Or, individual faculty members began carrying out their own solutions in their respective student groups, so that matters were settled differently by different professors and the nonagreement was tacitly allowed to stand. To the extent that he was identified as director of the program, Tussman made decisions that could be and were taken, by students and other faculty, as the course to be followed.

As in other of man's communal enterprises, there was only one moment when all the faculty was truly together: when they all met for the first time and agreed that they wished to participate in the ECP. After that, they were five individuals. There was an effort to develop a community, but, as with other faculties, there was a community of general purpose but seldom of method. Increasingly, Tussman emerged as the director of the program.

During the first year several crises among faculty, faculty and teaching assistants, and students and faculty were experienced and somehow surmounted. By the end of the year one member of the faculty, who committed himself for only one year, had to be replaced. In addition, another faculty member decided to leave the program, and all teachings assistants were told they would not be rehired. To replace the teaching assistants and the two faculty members, three new faculty members were added to the three who continued for the second year. It became evident that the idea of the ECP as conceived by Tussman was different from the ideas conceived by some of the others involved.

Three interrelated ideas are important to an understanding of Tussman's concept of the ECP and its progression during the first two years. First, and most basic, is his concept of the relationship of freedom and obligation. That is, that the members of any group having a specific purpose and organization of leadership, rules, and so on are free to exercise their rights by virtue of voluntarily assuming the obligation to follow the rules and the leadership agreed upon (Tussman, 1960). The second, but related, idea is that the quality of participation of each member of a democratic society depends on an education for public life which must have as its basis the theory of political obligation just stated (Tussman, 1960). Finally, the third and related idea is that the educator, being the professional, must decide on the form and content of the education of the future citizen, who, while in school, is considered to be a naive child (Tussman, 1967).

Thus, it would appear that when Tussman spoke of freedom, he thought that his students would learn to be free by learning the obligations of a free citizen—that is, to be responsible to leadership and rules. This was the central theme in the discourse in which he engaged his students during the two years, both in examination of the readings and also in general discussions.

The crises and changes in the program also tended to center around this theme. Conflict within the faculty often brought to light the implicit question of whether the faculty was free to develop the program—curriculum, interpretation of readings, and work requirements—according to its views or whether these things were to be decided in terms of the ideas of freedom and obligation. A majority of the faculty from both the first and second years was disappointed that a true collegial effort to create the program was not possible. They expected that such an effort would be a unique part of the program. Their experience was that efforts at working out plans together often were unsuccessful. Efforts to develop ideas about the curriculum independently were discouraged by Tussman. Increasingly during the two years, he found it necessary to make it plain that the program was not unplanned, that there was not freedom to follow individual wishes but that, on the contrary, there was a definite, uniform curriculum and plan of organization to be followed.

Most of the faculty point to one crisis as a salient representation of the conflict in the program. This occurred during the second semester, when Hobbes's *Leviathan* was being read. As with other readings, Tussman wished, through Hobbes's central ideas, to get across to the students the doctrine that it is necessary for citizens to obey the state. Not all the faculty agreed with this emphasis on the issue of how to be a good citizen. One member of the faculty (one of the two who left the program at the end of the first year) suggested that Hobbes be read as literature, in effect refusing to ask whether Hobbes's concept is true. Tussman used his authoritative position to insist that the question must be considered by students in doing this reading.

Similar events took place with the graduate student teaching assistants. All but one of them were several years along in their graduate studies. They came to the program highly recommended by their respective departments as scholars and teachers; because of their demonstrated excellence, they were selected from among a very able group of candidates by the program staff. Their initiation of contacts with students in the first week was disapproved by Tussman; their interest in participating in faculty planning was considered inappropriate and was met with expressed hostility and discouragement by him and varying degrees of lukewarm acknowledgement by most of the rest of the faculty. Their individual participation in the discussions in assigned seminars also was not welcomed by the faculty in most instances. But they had been selected presumably because of their superior abilities as young teachers and scholars; and the effect of the director's discouragement of any responsibilities outside the ordinary ones of a salaried reader was interpreted by the teaching assistants as demeaning and inconsistent with the promise offered by an experimental program.

There were several confrontations between faculty and students in the first year. Some students felt that the student body should participate in the determination of the curriculum. The faculty discussed with the students this issue and some aspects of the curriculum as well, but the decisions about the curriculum were reserved for the faculty. The faculty also refused the student's request to participate in regular faculty meetings. Finally, at the end of the first year, the students petitioned the faculty to give the teaching assistants the option of continuing in the program. The petition was rejected.

One nonacademic interaction illustrates the complexity and the difficulties of the relationships between the faculty and the students in a circumstance such as the ECP, where the experiment includes an attempt to work things out together. The interactions to be described concerned the furnishing of the house. At the outset the students had been told: "It's your house, your program." They also were given to understand that they could participate in planning the furnishing of the house, which, owing to poor planning by the administration, was not furnished at the opening of the semester. Only some wooden tables and straight-backed chairs had been available from the university warehouse. The students were eager to do something for their new home. In the early weeks they were heard to speculate on how to make this room or that nook a cozy place in which to sit and talk or read.

Some of the faculty spontaneously encouraged the students to organize a student government with committees to plan, among other things, the furnishing and decorating of the house. Such organizing was not decided upon by the faculty as a whole, and the students' efforts to organize themselves were not encouraged by Tussman. Informal suggestions to provide student art or student-wrought furniture, when funds were not available, were discouraged on the grounds that more comfortable and more elegant furnishings were necessary. The students' contributions to the expense of maintaining a coffee urn in the house were discontinued because Tussman felt that guests in his house should not have to pay for their coffee.

At the end of the first semester the chancellor's office made available about a thousand dollars to furnish the house. Tussman wished that the students would come to a consensus about the use of this money. In an effort to encourage them he, together with one other faculty member, arranged with the wife of a well-known professor who was not on the ECP faculty to act as advisor and treasurer for a house-furnishing-and-decorating committee of students. At one of the general meetings the students were told about the funds, and it was suggested that they select a committee. A number of girls volunteered to meet with the faculty wife. The meeting was a disaster. There were no more attempts to arrange another meeting. The faculty wife could not have been expected to anticipate the hostility or resentment with which the students greeted her. She attempted to conduct an orderly meeting amidst an unreceptive group. Not only were the students unable to cooperate with her suggestions, they also were unwilling to cooperate among themselves. She left bewildered and insulted; the remaining group divided, accusing each other of betraying the program, of poor taste, and so on. Those students who actively took part in the humiliation of the faculty wife considered her appointment by Tussman to be a direct statement of bad faith. The girls who had not received her appointment as an insult accused those who had of disrespect and outrageous behavior. Everyone was disappointed and angry.

Tussman and a majority of the staff accused the students of irresponsibility and bad manners. The students said the director was a tyrant, incapable of understanding mutuality, respect, and commitment. No one touched the house for a long time.

During the course of the second semester, a student who

lent his stereo equipment to the program removed it from the house. The people who used the house were desolate. Those students who still frequented the house and had, by this time, acquired an intimacy with each other and the secretary and two teaching assistants who also were more or less in residence prevailed on the secretary to attempt to maneuver the untouched funds toward the purchase of high-fi equipment. This was done with the knowledge of Tussman but without his permission. The high-fi and a rug, purchased a little later, were the only acquisitions made during the first year.

In the seminars, his students perceived Tussman as highly directive. One student, in an intellectual biography written at the end of the second year, expressed what many seemed to feel: "Professor Tussman's attitude toward his section seemed to be: 'You are young and stupid now; your opinions are for the most part worthless, for they have been built on emotion compounded with misinformation. You will listen to what I say and vehemently disagree in your insecurity, but perhaps five minutes later or five days or five years you will remember what I am saying and will admit that I am right. And I am not at all impatient. It will come, and I can wait.' "

After the end of the second year, all faculty involved in the program felt that the director had been dictatorial. They were surprised since that quality did not agree with their previous perceptions of him or with their understanding of the nature of the program. Some were bitter and felt they would not wish to engage in such an experiment again. But one member of the faculty expressed the opinion that the importance of Tussman's position and of the ECP was even greater because of the "anarchic challenge that we live with today. This program has a *raison d'être* that is not just education; it represents a commitment to a doctrine that is of special importance today."

How that doctrine (of freedom and responsibility) influenced the students is not entirely clear. We have some evidence, presented in Chapter Nine, that suggests the discussion of the issues may have contributed to the students' regarding their education in a personal and serious way. Many observations suggest that the students were more consistently and sharply aware of Tussman than of the other faculty and responded to his authoritative position either by admiring him for taking a stand or by disliking him for being dictatorial. Whichever way they saw him, their feelings about the program were that, indeed, it was Joe's College. In general, the faculty tended to agree.

One possible indirect effect, not of the concepts themselves but of the focus on the concepts considered of primary importance by Tussman, is the following: students who completed the program and who were considering a major in political science changed from that to another major in far greater proportion than did students in the regular program who planned to major in political science. (The difference is statistically significant at the .05 level.) Perhaps the intense focus on one concept of political man sated their interest and led to their pursuit of studies in other fields.

All students perceived the program as having one quality, and that was freedom. With few exceptions the students felt that they were free to pursue their interests in the manner of their choosing. With few exceptions they perceived Tussman as allowing them that freedom, whether they ended their second year critical of the program, praising it, or indifferent to it. These different attitudes often were related to how the students responded to freedom. Some of their perceptions of and responses to the freedom are evident in the following excerpts from their intellectual biographies.

The most valuable part of the program for me was the almost excessive amount of time given the student and the relatively complete freedom regarding attendance and assignments. We were left in a position to do whatever we liked, whenever we liked. For me this meant a number of things. At times it meant doing little or none of the reading, not doing papers, not going to lectures. It meant doing photography as intensely as I wanted. I frankly don't think I would have been able to realize whatever aptitude I may have for photography had I not been able to work at it, at times to the exclusion of almost all else. Another aspect of the freedom given me was the time to think things out—things that had nothing to do with school and photography. . . . If nothing else that freedom was invaluable in terms of getting adjusted to a rather drastic change in environment. It seems that Professor Tussman saw the value of time to do nothing but think and in fact made that time available.

The setting was not so much positive as nonnegative—as little interference as possible.

I did not think that learning about this or that was the object of the program, rather, a specialized kind of experience wherein the student is allowed tremendous amounts of unorganized time in which to develop, in his own way, his intellectual habits and to confront himself, his character, his desire, his future, and his past free from the pressures and confusions of the degree-directed university. . . . This statement is something of a post facto *rationalization for not having been very successful in dealing with the core material. I would probably say that I have not done very much in two years at the EC. The material which did engross me was outside the program, cultural anthropology.*

My first reaction was to throw up my books, go swimming. I did not have any grades or tests to worry about, passing the course seemed a cinch. . . . I could not be comfortable. I realized I could not turn my back on my intellectual self while being within an educational metaphor. . . . A new viewpoint arose. . . . I wanted to study for my own improvement; indeed I became zealous to understand myself in every possible context.

We have had time to form the intense personal relationships which have proved to be the vehicle from which I have learned the most. Talking and visiting with friends has been my major pastime here, subordinating in influence and importance both studying and reading. . . . Because I have so little compulsory work, it has been correspondingly more difficult for me to escape thinking about myself; . . . it has produced a greater degree of honesty in us.

The gift of free time was unexpected, unexplained, undirected, and unwanted. The assigned work I did gladly, but it gave me little satisfaction because it was not demanding. . . . It was just the same as high school.

There is much I want to do. I finally can bring myself to practice the piano two to four hours a day. And composing. Nothing may come of it, but it will be a pleasure to find out.

The Tussman program allows the student a great deal of freedom, and I feel freedom is something which presupposes responsibility. Lack of this responsibility is the main reason many students, including myself, found it hard to acclimate themselves to such a different academic atmosphere. More frequent and more definite writing assignments would be my first recommendation and Tuesday, Thursday periods should accommodate those who wish to participate actively and those who wish to follow the line of discussion.

In brief, although Tussman held a firm position to the effect that the teacher knows best, at the same time, through both the design and accident of the program, there was generated an atmosphere of almost total freedom for the student. Some of them used it, some wasted it, and some resented it.

At the outset everyone in the program, faculty and students alike, no doubt had expectations and intentions of accomplishing a great deal of satisfying work. All faculty and many students were mainly disappointed in that expectation, and their disappointment influenced the difficulties of implementing a central idea of the program: the faculty plan of providing the students with ample time to read and reread their texts and to think about them and ponder their own responses. No doubt the faculty hoped, privately, that the students, freed after years of restriction by public school systems, would respond to their freedom with a release of energy and work with interest, enthusiasm, and intense involvement after accommodating to the new climate and learning how to use their freedom. However, they undoubtedly extended their laissez-faire attitude far beyond their own capacities to tolerate it. Students did not complete readings in the ample time provided nor did they complete written assignments in reasonable time. Eventually, faculty anxiety rose sharply, and they may have feared encouraging anarchy in the young students. The next occasion perhaps was followed by an attempt at discipline, perhaps by chiding and a lecture on the relationship of responsibility and freedom.

Such experiences, repeated periodically by students and faculty, no doubt eroded their earlier intentions and expectations of great accomplishments. One can imagine a professor backing off, distressed at his distrust of his students and of his own principles. The students either complied, feeling it was the same old system, or, more likely, backed off from their teacher by rebelling and further challenging his principles. It is no wonder that students' impressions of the program varied from "total freedom" to "dictatorship" and that the faculty often was demoralized, keenly disappointed in their experiment.

Perhaps a similar state of affairs prevailed at times when Tussman and his colleagues differed. That is, Tussman may have expected that by his not insisting on his point of view the others eventually would agree. When the expectation was not fulfilled, a firm director seemed necessary to keep the program on an even keel. As with the students, dismay and retreat from each other on the part of all concerned easily could follow.

The students created another part of the atmosphere of the program. They appeared to yearn for fraternity among themselves, even more than did the faculty members. They looked to each other for acceptance and friendship; they looked to the program as an opportunity to transcend themselves and their knowledge of the mundane. In short, all its constituents hoped the program would transcend the banality of ordinary experience. Much friction occurring during the first year grew out of the fact that in the minds of the faculty this transcendence was to be confined to the classroom and the ordinary relationships deriving from it, whereas the students desired to achieve a fraternity among themselves and their instructors—to live as cherished individuals in a community of teachers and students, working together to achieve the good life and a more perfect wisdom.

As a result of this desire, unexpressed and untapped, about thirty students unofficially became the keepers and caretakers of the house. The remaining students fell into two general groupings: one was seen and known in the house, although it did not attempt to become attached to the house; and another was neither seen nor known. The latter group was the largest. They were silent in meetings and, for the most part, in seminars. They were undistinguished.

They were known by name to few of the faculty and teaching assistants. In effect, their existence in the common life of the program extended no farther than the enrollment list. The group known, but not there, was comprised of students who were not personally attached to the fate of the program; however, they did participate in the classroom: they spoke in meetings, expressed their views, and contributed to the academic life.

The group which contributed most to the academic life of the program was the one most intensely concerned with its communal life. They attached themselves informally to each other and the program. In varying degrees, they identified with the fate and shape of the program. In effect, they took over the house, leaving their personal belongings as tangible evidence of their occupation. Their casual mode, unconventional style, and unpredictable moods alienated them as a group from the orderly majority. Some students complained that the occupation of the house by this exclusive group precluded other groups' enjoying the facilities and space of the house. Many students sought refuge in the established fraternities; others found congenial friendships outside the house.

The group that did develop in the house in an unplanned and spontaneous way could not be identified as "Greek"; its members did not enjoy the explicit bonds of fraternity or sorority but were, nevertheless, looking for each other and for something else. This group could not appropriately be called a community. It was less orderly than a community, less self-conscious or exclusive. It was informal; members recognized each other as individuals rather than as members of the same group. The group also existed without expressed purpose. It was simply identifiable individuals who happened to be at a particular place at a particular time and were known to each other.

This group also served as a human weather vane for the program: its members were, on the whole, the most sensitive to changes in faculty mood. They responded most directly and immediately to faculty overtures; they attempted to form an articulate student opinion; they were present more than others; they affected events dramatically. They were at once the most committed to the program and, also, the most troublesome. They were most loved and feared.

No doubt a handful of students from this group at the house on the last day of the first year of the program were responsible for the grotesque sculpture which survived them at the end of the day. It stood like a huge Goliath in the middle of the commons room. Its body was an intricately balanced concept of library chair upon library chair, projecting precariously from floor to ceiling. It stood their mysteriously, threatening at any moment to topple to the ground. On the walls of the room, students had tacked embittered eulogies and poems to the director, expressions of traditional ambivalence toward the teacher.

In the second year the program was not as turbulent and lively as in the first. Although they met and worked together throughout the year, from the start the new faculty members were not united into a group as was the first faculty. Ways of working together as well as the conflicts that developed in the first year were carried over into the second. The new members introduced some new harmony and new differences. Perhaps because of the first year turbulence, Tussman made it clear that the overall program took precedence over individual faculty wishes and predilections, and, in so doing, he became identifiable as director of the program. Faculty members tended to feel themselves individuals, functioning separately from the others and, in several instances, relating to their students more closely than to each other. They more easily set aside ideas discussed in faculty meetings and tended to introduce their ideas in their seminars and to relate readings to their and their students' interests. The new faculty felt that the morale of the students was poor; without the background provided by the preliminary faculty discussions and the first year of the program, they felt that the students were in the habit of doing very little work and that they had little interest in changing that pattern. Efforts at rejuvenating student interest were made by inroducing new readings and by appeals to the students' interests, however far removed from the themes of the program. The new faculty even suspected that some students had frankly cynical attitudes and were staying in the program, although having little regard for it, in order to avoid the draft or the lower division requirements. In their work they felt the students showed an interest primarily in expressing their own feelings and reactions, albeit in a very creative fashion, and had little interest in analytical thinking or writing. All in all, they felt that personality differences in staff and in the student body precluded any communal effort and limited the work accomplished during the year.

A final constraint on the spirit of the program was imposed by a revision of the curriculum planned for the last half of the second year. The original plan called for a study of the contemporary racial revolution in America, to be undertaken by means of direct student observations of the community, its institutions, and its current problems. It was to culminate the study of previous periods of change and was an opportunity to examine some of the curricular themes by participant observation in the student's own civilization. The faculty, concerned that the students' inquiries would prove too challenging to local institutions and government, feared they would be turning the students loose on the community rather than launching a scholarly inquiry. The plan was dropped and instead the students were required to devote their last period of study to the writing of an intellectual autobiography.

The students, disappointed in this last assignment, lost enthusiasm for the program and sensed that, perhaps with the exception of Tussman and one or two others, the faculty had lost interest in teaching, being occupied with their own interests or intramural conflicts. A number of students expressed the feeling that the program, as an integrated academic enterprise, slowed to a halt in the last half of the second year. They became involved in activities and interests elsewhere. Nevertheless, about half continued attending scheduled meetings and seminars regularly and responding to work assignments.

The faculty and some students felt a strong urge to achieve a collegial atmosphere, a fraternity, and a community. In this effort they can be seen, in retrospect, to be like a family. While feeling strong bonds and attempting to unite in a mutual enterprise, they experienced strong ambivalence. The much coveted closeness was accompanied by feelings of anxiety: there was the possibility of loss of independence, the danger of being coopted. Unexpected and surprising competitions, animosities, and jealousies sprang up to disrupt and thwart the harmony that seemed near to achievement. But such is the human condition. The regret is that these experi-

ences when they occur in an academic or work setting and sometimes in a family are considered to lie outside the sphere of learning.
Retrospectively, it seems these personal and occasionally painful
experiences of the faculty and students might have provided answers
for some questions raised by the curriculum: what is freedom? what
is responsibility?

Chapter 5

Personality Development in the College Experience

*W*hat, after all, are the effects of the college experience and how are they to be evaluated? Considering the increasing number of people in our society who assume and seek its benefits, the need to develop answers to this question grows more urgent. Important economic consequences are an accepted fact: it is well known that a college graduate can anticipate an overall annual income that is predictably several thousand dollars higher than that of a high school graduate. However, neither economic consequences nor the development of scientific or scholarly proficiency are under consideration. I am writing, rather, of effects of a more general sort: of the general development of the person as one interested in taking the responsibility for the direction of his own life and for the quality of life—his own as well as those of others in his society. These effects are not necessarily represented by the student's college record: the courses he has taken, his grade point average, the graduate record exam, and other criteria of certification. They are the effects which the liberal educator sets as his goals.

Meiklejohn defines the goal of liberal education as follows: "The liberal college . . . intends to build up in a student the power of self-direction in the affairs of life. It rests upon the assumption, or the assertion, that over against the specialized teaching of men for banking, for scholarship, for industry, for art, for medicine, for law, and the like, there is the general teaching of men for intelligence in the conduct of their own lives as human individuals" (1932, p. 6).

Tussman expresses similar goals for the Experimental College Program at Berkeley: the cultivation of human understanding "to fit us for the life of active membership in the democratic community; to fit us to serve, in its broadest sense, our common political vocation (1969, pp. 3–4).

Insofar as it has a unifying theme and purpose, the lower division program in the College of Letters and Science of the university has the goal of providing a general education. By means of required curriculum, the Letters and Science program attempts to develop analytic power within the student, sensitivity, and tolerance. It endeavors to broaden the student's understanding of himself and of his social world. This goal is partly a goal of the curriculum and partly it is expected to ensue from the educational process itself as well as from activities and the atmosphere of the university community. Aside from the stimulation of new ideas and concepts, the personal engagement with faculty and other students is expected to enrich the personal development of the individual.

In what terms are we to evaluate the achievement of such goals? Ideally, we would study the life styles of graduates of various colleges and attempt to relate them to the college experience: a complex undertaking. Freedman (1967) has reported studies of alumni at Vassar College which suggest that certain attitudes emerging during the college years may endure throughout the person's lifetime. However, such far-ranging studies are rare. More frequently psychologists' efforts have been directed to the study of personal development during the college years, focusing on changes in attitudes and values.

Typically, in these studies, attitudes, opinions, and preferences of students are periodically evaluated, changes are noted, and these attitudinal changes are used to infer changes in the personality. Personality is defined here as a relatively unique patterning of processes whereby a human organizes his experiences and his actions in the world, a patterning which makes it possible for us to recognize one person as different from another and to be able to recognize the same person in separate points in time, despite different actions in different contexts. These are processes of living: biological, for example, a person's level of arousal and energy; social, such as a person's social context, his attitudes, values, and ways of relating to himself and to other social beings; and ego processes, for example, capacities for integrating new experiences with old and capacities for functioning, including intellectual capacities. These personality changes may be regarded as developmental, that is, they result in a more highly developed person. Sanford, in considering personality change, makes a distinction between growth and development:

Growth may be defined simply as expansion of the personality—the addition of parts (e.g., habits, needs, or beliefs) and the enlargement of existing parts (e.g., an increase in the intensity of a need). If we conceive of personality as a system, we may regard its growth in the same way that we regard the growth of any other system (a city, a university, or a department of a university). Growth may or may not be "healthy," in the sense of being favorable to the over-all functioning of the system; it may be malignant. . . .

Development means, most essentially, the organization of increasing complexity. For example, a child behaves in an all-or-nothing fashion because his personality is very much all of one piece. With time, various sub-systems become differentiated and take on particular functions; and without losing their particular identity, these sub-systems become integrated into larger wholes in order to serve the larger purposes of the organism (1967).

Development, as I use the term here, refers to an increase in the complexity and level of integration of the personality. For example, the college freshman tends to be relatively dependent on authority, especially adult authority, for definition and interpretation of his experiences. He seeks hard, stable facts about life and the world so that he may use them to guide his way in life. As he progresses through late adolescence (and presumably, as a result— at least in part—of his educational experience), he becomes increasingly aware that stable facts are scarce, and, at the same time, he learns to rely on his own subjective judgment for making decisions for action in the world. If his development follows this general pattern, he changes from the experience of self as object responding to absolute authority (what does the teacher want me to know?) to a subjective self-experience accompanied by a sense of increasing independence and self-reliance (what do I want to know?). His personality may now include new (or clearly defined) elements: values that are a basis for choices for action and the disposition to choose—a disposition that encompasses attitudes toward the self as a maker of choices; in other words, ego attitudes. Within the whole personality these elements require a new, more complex, and higher level of integration. (The young man described as a game player in Chapter Ten illustrates these changes.)

Such observations of development in college have been made frequently. The earliest systematic observations, made at Vassar during the 1950s under the auspices of the Mary Conover Mellon Foundation, produced a number of measures for the empirical study of attitudes which relate to these changes. They were, notably, the Developmental Status Scale, the Impulse Expression Scale, and the Social Maturity Scale, all of which can be used to demonstrate differences between freshmen and seniors (Freedman, 1967, Chapter 3). These measures have been modified and are included in a comprehensive set of scales, the Omnibus Personality Inventory (OPI), which was developed at the Center for Research and Development in Higher Education, University of California, Berkeley. Of the thirteen scales in Form C of the OPI, seven emphasizing personality qualities (as distinguished from qualities of cognitive functioning) were used in this study. The scales are described in detail in Appendix C. The OPI has been used for a variety of studies of student personality and development. For example, Katz (1968) administered scales from the OPI to the same students as freshmen and as seniors. The personality scale changes that took place were reported as increases in measures of Social Maturity, Developmental Status, Impulse Expression, and Estheticism, and decreases in measures of Ethnocentrism, Authoritarianism and in Social Alienation. These results were interpreted to mean that the students were moving toward greater open-mindedness, tolerance, and recognition of the complexity of the world. The scores of seniors reflected an increase in spontaneity, appreciation of a variety of artistic and aesthetic experiences, and they suggested greater willingness to experiment with new ways of action in their personal behavior. Their scores also suggested that they achieved greater freedom from social conventions and stereotyped views of right and wrong and were more able to accept diversity in humans. One could infer that they moved both toward an integration of feelings and thoughts and toward greater acceptance of themselves and of others. These are some of the qualities that can be used as indicators of the intelligence defined by Meiklejohn as the goal of a liberal education.

These personality scales begin an effort to evaluate the larger effects of education. They are limited. One problem is that questionnaires always reflect the questionnaire's reality, not necessarily that of the respondent. In other words, the view of the student is confined to attitudes included in the questionnaire. Another difficulty is that each scale defines only one particular dimension (such as expression of impulse, orientation to authority, and esthetic interest) so that only these particular attitudinal dimensions are considered. A limit is also introduced by the fact that the student is asked to respond to relative statements ("I like to read about artistic or literary achievements"; "I have often gone against my parents' wishes"; "I like to flirt") with an absolute answer (True or False). No contextual conditions can be imposed that might add the dimension of meaning.

Within these limits the measures serve the purpose for which they were constructed: that is, to differentiate groups of college students at different levels of development. Initially, the scales were constructed to evaluate developmental differences between groups of freshmen and seniors in order to study changes taking place over the four college years. The scales are sufficiently sensitive so that they also can differentiate developmental groups at any point during the college period. For example, we were able to use them to define differences between the freshman students who applied to the Experimental College Program and those who opted for the regular program (Chapter Three). We undertook to use this method with such differentiation in mind.

The students in our study responded to our scales at the beginning of their freshman year and at the end of their sophomore year. (These scales were the same as those used by Katz in his studies.) In this two-year period our entire sample, taken as a whole (both men and women in the entire group), showed score differences that are significant at the .01 level of confidence. As in Katz's four-year comparison, our students' scores were higher (at the end of two years) in such measures as Social Maturity, Impulse Expression, and Developmental Status, and they were lower in Ethnocentrism and Authoritarianism. In our research report we stated (Suczek and Alfert, 1970):

The direction of these changes is consistent with the idea of personality development characterized by increase in complexity of personality; there is a greater tolerance for differences, an increase in diversity of interests, feelings and impulses are more available to awareness and more appropriately expressed, and there is a corresponding decrease of inhibition. The individual student making such a change is more free to use his imagination and depends less on convention and stereotype in dealing with people. Female students express less feeling of alienation and social isolation than they did as freshmen. Male students express more awareness of their feelings; they are less dependent on an image of themselves that stresses masculine stereotypes; i.e., they no longer feel the necessity to present themselves as "he-men."

These changes can be inferred from the differences in personality scale scores. They are abstractions based on the average difference in scores for the entire group and therefore represent an "average" student or, more correctly, an average of students' characteristics.

Every teacher knows that a freshman class is composed of students with a wide range of individual development. Each student is unique. Some are clearly adolescent, while others are essentially adult in their level of development. Thus, it is reasonable to assume that the students who began at different levels of development changed at different rates or in different degrees. The scatter of scores for our group of freshmen did demonstrate that the students were starting college at different points in their development. We therefore grouped students together according to their initial scores and two years later found no significant difference in changes achieved by the various groups. Since we know from personal observation that students do change differentially, this latter finding may be related to a limitation of our measures or the way we used them; that is, we may not be able to make such fine discriminations with measures used this way.

The general direction of change, however, was similar to that described for the whole sample. These changes reflected an adaptation to the university climate and the Berkeley student atmosphere, including an emulation by the beginning student of the ideal image he perceived in the more advanced students. This image, I believe, was based on the idea—then typically held by students—that a young person in college is in the process of reevaluating the attitudes and values he acquired in eighteen previous years of acculturation, a process involving the discard of conservative attitudes and the adoption of more liberal ones.

Observation through interviews with individual students suggested that some changed scores reflected a conscious effort to adopt such an image, whereas for other students, the scores reflected a basic developmental change taking place. (More discussion will be devoted to these and other aspects of change in the later chapters of this book.)

Thus far it has been shown that the students in our study, taken as a whole, showed the same overall pattern of development that was described in previous studies. The fundamental question—

whether a difference in development can be associated with a difference in two educational atmospheres—still remains. To answer this question, we considered first the students who had been chosen for the ECP and those who volunteered but were not chosen. At the outset these two groups achieved nearly identical measurements on our scales. At the end of the second year there were no significant differences between them in the amount of change made by each group according to personality scale scores. In brief, these two groups of students began at the same level of development and made essentially the same amount of changes, although they were in different educational settings.

The results were somewhat different when the Experimental College students were compared with regular lower division students who were not interested in the program. These two groups had significantly different scores at the outset. Furthermore, although their final scores show no significant differences, the regular college group did make many significantly greater changes—a factor which must be taken into account when noting the similarity of the end-scores between the Experimental College and the regular lower division groups. Essentially, what took place was a leveling of differences. For example, on the Developmental Status Scale both groups changed in the same direction. The change for the regular college group was greater, but that group began with a lower mean score. Thus, at the end of two years the Experimental College group still had a higher score, but the difference between the two groups no longer was significant. However, of the remaining differences at the end of two years, men in the ECP still were significantly more strongly oriented to esthetic interests and activities. By comparison, men in the regular program expressed increased interest in science and problem solving (dealing with quantities and absolutes) and were much less likely to acknowledge feelings of anxiety or of personal inadequacy.

Women students in the Experimental Program also continued to demonstrate different attitudes when compared with women in the regular program. Essentially, these differences suggested that their level of development remained more complex as compared with the level of those in the regular program. The women in the ECP were more independent socially, more flexible, and more tolerant both of their own foibles and weaknesses and those of others.

In general the students who preferred the regular lower division program started, as a group, at a less complex level of development (as defined by our personality scales) and had, therefore, a greater distance to travel along developmental dimensions as defined by these scales. As a result, their strides appeared greater than those taken by the Experimental College group. Each group inevitably included individuals who differed markedly in their level of development at the outset. If we assume that the experiences of individuals in the two programs were different, it is necessary to compare individuals in the two groups who were similar in their scores at the outset.

Comparison of the mean change on the scales over two years by groups matched on the basis of their beginning scores showed only a slight difference in the degree of change made by students in the two educational atmospheres. Only one scale reflected a significant difference in mean change: according to the F scale (Authoritarianism), students in the Experimental College Program changed more than students similar to them who were in the regular program ($p < .05$). In both groups, as might be expected from previous research made by Plant (1965), showing a general diminution of attitudes oriented to absolute authority, sharp in-group-out-group distinctions, and the like, the change was in the direction of a lower mean score. In other words, students in the ECP changed to a more relativistic outlook.

The various analyses completed at this point in the study indicated, on the basis of these scales, no substantial difference in development between students in the Experimental College Program and those in the regular college program. It appears that a major influencing factor was the student's level of development at time of entrance into college. The data suggested that among students whose development indicated greater complexity more were inclined to choose an experimental program, where they continued the same course of development. Among the students of less complex development, more were inclined to choose the conventional program, where they made considerable developmental changes. The individuals who developed in either of these two cases most frequently were active in campus life both in and out of the academic sphere, although this apparently was not a necessary condition for their development.

The only conclusion to be drawn from the work thus far appears to be that during the first two years of the program the developmental changes markedly tended to decrease differences that existed at the time of entrance. This outcome, suggesting a kind of homogenization, is unlikely to satisfy the educator who is interested in the development of all his students. Nor is it an outcome that would satisfy any observer of individual human development. Development of the personality is a complex and many-faceted process, and it seems unlikely that a leveling of differences is an adequate statement of what took place. Nor does it seem likely that there were no differences between the experiences of students in the two settings. It is more reasonable to assume that either our measurements or the manner in which we used them were unsuited to the task. As a matter of fact, both assumptions appear to be correct.

First, each scale we used is one dimensional; it can be used to represent a change in the characteristic it measures (for example, impulse expression) ranging in degree from some point below to some point above the average of any given group. It does not, however, demonstrate qualitative change. Similarly, use of the scales in combination to define a large entity such as overall complexity of development also produced a quantitative, linear measure that apparently did not define the appropriate qualities in our changing students. For instance, using combinations of scales we matched the more developed and less developed in the two different conditions at time of entrance so as to compare development in respect to those conditions, and we found no substantial difference. As we studied the problem, we discovered other important student characteristics that were not measured by the scales but which were important to development in each of the two atmospheres. By defining the students simply in terms of their initial scores, we left out dimensions of major relevance to the students' interaction with the educational structure.

We discovered, in other words, that our concept of the students, as defined by our scales, was too simple. In addition, we discovered that our concept of what constitutes the student's educational atmosphere also was too simple: neither the Experimental College Program nor the regular lower division program was such a unitary entity as our method of comparison assumed it to be (see Chapters Nine and Ten).

The problem of evaluating the effects of the college experience therefore remains. Our study, like previous research, demonstrates that developmental changes occur during college years. Such developmental changes, involving fundamental attributes of the whole person, may be taken to be reasonable analogues of the kind of development the liberal educator hopes to stimulate in his students. How such development may be related to the student's later life we still do not know. This is a subject for further study.

Of more immediate relevance is the question of how such development is related to the educational experience itself. Again, as in our study, most research shows an overall relationship between the college experience and personality development. Which specific aspects of development are related to which specific aspects of the college experience remains unclear. This uncertainty has been interpreted by some as possibly indicating a failure of the educational structure itself. Axelrod and others summarize a number of studies which "show that neither professors nor courses appeared to be among the major influences" (1969, p. 52). As I already implied, it is my contention that the lack of evidence of any connection may be due to a failure of the research method rather than to an actual lack of connection. Professors and courses may not be appropriate units of analysis.

Chapter 6

Developmental Change in Response to Challenge

*T*he task of devising college environments and programs intended to maximize personal development is as complex as the process of human life itself. As educators, we tend to differ—sometimes widely—on basic goals: what aspects of growth and development we wish to emphasize. We also disagree concerning methods to best encourage personal growth. Moreover, the young person coming to college already has been engaged in a process of becoming for nearly two decades. He has well established his patterns of learning, how he perceives the world, and how he

68

organizes his experiences. What aspects of such a developmental process are we best able to enhance? Finally, each student is a palpable and unique self, easily distinguished from all the separate and unique others. Even if one were to ignore the uncertainty and disagreement among educators in the matter of both ends and means, what kind of a program can facilitate all these different processes of development at the same time?

The questions centering about what aspects of the college program relate to the developmental process also are complex. Is it the content, the structure, or the individual instructor? Or is it each of these elements in the general atmosphere of the whole college? If we change a part, what happens to the whole? These questions are of interest both for developmental psychology and for educational planning. They have specific relevance to the contemporary issue of whether students should have more choice in shaping their educational experience.

In the previous chapter I discussed work demonstrating some general effects of the college experience on development. Empirical investigations of effects of specific aspects of the educational process, however, have been relatively few. An early study by Newcomb (1943) at Bennington demonstrated some connections between aspects of the college environment and changes in students' attitudes. Attitudes and value orientations of students were found to change in the direction of those identified with prestige-endowed individuals in the college community. More recent studies of residential college programs at the University of Michigan (Newcomb and others, 1970) demonstrate a similar process of accentuation. Newcomb's theory of accentuation predicts that, in appropriate environments, students initially high on a measure of a trait will score still higher than those initially lower on the same trait.

Research typically indicates some of the more general consequences of the overall educational process. For example, both the study by Katz (1968) and the initial evaluation of the pre- and postmeasures used in this study demonstrate a general tendency for complexity and flexibility of the personality to increase during the college experience. Such effects have been well demonstrated in numerous studies (Sanford, 1962c; Feldman and Newcomb, 1969). There still is relatively little understanding, however, regarding the particular aspects of the educational process important to the facilitation of such change.

One theory we use to try to understand the general process of personality change assumes that change begins when the individual is challenged to respond in a new way. If his habitual form of response is not appropriate to the situation, he must generate new responses. This theory is set forth by Wheelis (1950) and later is stated elaborately by him (1969). The same principle in neonatal development also is described by Frank (1966, Chapter 2). The process of development I described in the previous chapter is facilitated in a similar fashion. For change to take place, however, the challenge must not be overwhelming; and, furthermore, the individual must be psychologically ready to perceive and respond to the challenge (Sanford, 1962b). A more elaborate statement later is made by Sanford, who concludes: "What the state of readiness means, most essentially, is that the individual is now open to new kinds of stimuli and prepared to deal with them in an adaptive way" (1967, p. 54). As new behavior is repeated and becomes integrated into the personality it becomes a new "part," and the previous personality organization is modified accordingly. Theoretically, as the process continues the person becomes more complex; he develops more possibilities for undertaking more and different kinds of actions and more vantage points for contemplating the world and organizing his experiences.

In this study there was opportunity to evaluate developmental change and its relationship to challenge as experienced in the educational structure. We had so far failed—in our systematic studies—to demonstrate any specific connection between the academic experience and developmental change. The theory I sketched leads to a different kind of evaluation of our data. Previously, we followed a procedure whereby we established the student's developmental level at time of entering college; next we determined the degrees of change made by students categorized according to their initial levels of development. The result of experience in two different atmospheres appeared to be a leveling out of initial differences.

For our new strategy, we decided we needed to identify characteristics of the academic atmosphere that might challenge the student. It would then be possible to measure the student's subsequent development in relation to the degree of challenge provided in each milieu. My colleague Elizabeth Alfert suggested a redefinition of the student in terms of the degree of structure he was accustomed to in his life prior to college. This redefinition made the new evaluation possible.

In all, three variables needed to be defined: the student's characteristic way of functioning, the quality of the academic structure (in terms of the way of functioning it required of the student), and developmental change.

Developmental change we defined simply as an increasing complexity of the personality and an increasing flexibility of functioning. Changes in complexity and flexibility were inferred from patterns of scores on several personality measures. The measures included the Authoritarianism and Ethnocentrism scales presented in Adorno, Frankel-Brunswick, Levinson, and Sanford (1950); and three scales from the Omnibus Personality Inventory (1962). Although each measure separately defines a specific personality characteristic, taken together they represent a summary of the general characteristics in which we were interested. We next assumed that the quality of the student's previous life situation was of central importance in the development of his characteristic way of functioning. We defined quality of life situation by using the family religious affiliation as a criterion, considering its structural dimensions a continuum from a relatively unstructured to a relatively structured style of living. Finally, we defined the quality of the educational structure in college in similar terms: relatively structured or relatively unstructured.

Previous work has made clear that people belonging to different religious groups tend to differ in certain personality characteristics as well as in family life style. Carlson (1934) found that religious affiliation is an important basis for differentiating attitudes of undergraduate students. Defining conservatism as adherence to the existing order and opposition to its change, he found Jewish students the most liberal when compared with Protestants and Catholics. They were most likely to oppose prohibition; they were sympathetic to pacifism, to communism, and to birth control; and they believed least in "the reality of God." Roscoe (1968) similarly found Jewish college students more liberal than were Christians;

Harris (1932) found students with no religious affiliation less conservative than those with church preference; and Allport (1954) found less ethnic prejudice among nonchurchgoers.

These findings suggest that young people with a Christian religious background tend to take a more structured view of the world and that, conversely, young people of non-Christian background—that is, agnostic or Jewish—tend to a relatively less structured view of the world.

A clear explication of this congruence as it relates to family experience is made by Haan, and others (1968), in a study of the moral reasoning of young adults. In describing young people characterized by different kinds of morality, Haan and her co-workers used religious affiliation of the family as a descriptive variable to define three groups. In the first of these, upbringing in agnostic homes and in homes with no formal religion was found to be characterized by fathers who encouraged their sons to try new things, and by general parental permissiveness. These parents also encouraged children to make their own choices as much as possible. Members of a second group, from atheistic or Jewish backgrounds, had homes in which children apparently were indulged. There was a lack of predictability in their lives, and clarification of rights and responsibilities also was lacking. In contrast to these two groups was the third, whose religious upbringing was in affiliation with Protestantism or Catholicism. They are described as conducting their lives more conservatively and in ways conforming to traditional expectations. In their homes they tended to be more influenced by their parents than were members of other groups, and they experienced clear rules, enforced by predictable patterns of punishments and rewards.

On the basis of the consistency of these observations we identified two groups in our sample: the first (coming from families affiliated with either a Protestant or a Catholic religious orientation) was defined as having had a relatively structured family life experience. The second (coming from families that were Jewish, agnostic, or lacking in religious affiliation) was defined as coming from a relatively unstructured family life experience. We assumed that the structure, or lack of it, would be broadly but characteristically experienced in family life, although the focus of such experience would be especially sharp in the interactions of parent and child.

Representatives of these two groups of students were found in both educational atmospheres. The primary qualitative difference between these atmospheres was the degree of structure. The lower division program provided the more structured educational atmosphere. Although some educational innovation attempting to introduce more choice for the student began during that period, the overall design of the lower division program emphasized the fulfillment of certain requirements. The result was an atmosphere of limited choice. The lower division courses had a format of lectures and required reading as well as a schedule of quizzes, midterm, and final examinations which structured the schedule and focus of the reading. Grades—both for examinations and for the whole course— reinforced this scheduling and the educational emphasis on "what is one expected to do" or "what does the teacher want." For many students, at least during their first year, academic work took up the bulk of their time.

The Experimental College Program attempted to provide an educational program with an untraditional structure. The program intended to emphasize personal interaction and collaboration between students and faculty and to maximize freedom for the student to take responsibility for his own work. Instead of content being arbitrarily divided into academic fields and courses of one semester duration, the program devoted two years to the study of four periods of crisis and change in Western civilization. The working method included readings from primary sources and general discussions—in small seminars—of the readings and the ideas they stimulated. Occasional papers were required and were discussed extensively by the faculty seminar leaders, either in written commentary or in individual meetings with the students. There were no regularly scheduled lectures, no examinations, and no grades. A leisurely and contemplative atmosphere was encouraged; there students presumably were free to develop their own paces and pursue interests arising from the program studies.

Five of the ten personality measures included in the study were used for defining development. Students were classified as "developed" or "not developed" according to two different procedures. The first took into account the change in each of their personality scale scores. A student was judged "developed" if the pattern of his test scores showed a change from less to more complex and from conventional and inhibited forms of behavior to more flexible and appropriate expressions of the self (see Appendix C).

The proportion of students classified "developed" was nearly the same in the group coming from a Protestant and Catholic background (54%) and in the group coming from Jewish or agnostic family backgrounds (52%). However, the two groups showed a different pattern of development in the two academic settings.

Students coming from a "structured" family experience, if they were in the "structured" program (regular lower division), showed development less frequently (46%), whereas if they were in the "unstructured" program (ECP) they showed development more frequently (66%), or, $X^2 = 4.60$, df 1, $p < .05$. The opposite was the case for students from an unstructured family experience. The latter students, if they were in the unstructured program, developed comparatively less often (45%) than if they were in the structured program (56%).

Furthermore, when students from a structured background and those from an unstructured background were compared in the unstructured program, the students from a structured background were classified as "developed" significantly more often than were the others ($X^2 = 3.26$, df 1, $p > .10$). In other words, a student who grew up in a relatively structured family atmosphere was more likely to develop in the unstructured educational atmosphere than was a student coming from an unstructured experience (for whom there was continuity rather than change in this regard).

The second procedure for determining "development" and "nondevelopment" was undertaken to account for the differences in student levels of development at the time of their first response to the personality measures. Students in the four subgroups (structured background—structured program; structured background—unstructured program; unstructured background—structured program; unstructured background—unstructured program) were matched in terms of the level of their averaged first test score (see Appendix C) as well as in terms of the pattern of the initial scores. Only students in the unstructured experimental program and those who applied but were not chosen in the random selection process were used in this analysis because of relative similarity in initial test scores and patterns in these two groups. Twenty-one individuals in each of the four subgroups were found to correspond closely in respect to original score patterns. Using the final scores, an evaluation (an analysis of variance) was made to compare developmental changes.

The students from a structured background in the unstructured program showed greater gains in complexity than did the same kind of students in the structured program ($t = 2.36$, df 40, $p < .05$). Also, students from a structured background developed more than did students from an unstructured background in the experimental program ($t = 2.28$, df 40, $p < .05$), while there was a tendency for the students from an unstructured background to show greater development than the others in the structured program ($t = 1.69$, df 40, $p < .10$). Furthermore, taken as a whole, the interaction between background of the student and the structure of the program can be shown to be significant ($F = 7.45$, df 1/80, $p < .01$).

This part of the study was intended to clarify the relationship between the student's development as a person and the experience provided by the college—to consider what aspects of the college experience are important, what aspects of the student's personality and background are important, and in what way they can interact to facilitate development. The interest, in other words, lies in the interaction between the student's past environment—in which he has developed his perspective of the world, his expectations and modes of action—and the college environment. Such interaction generally has been studied in terms of substantive attitudes and values, change being defined in terms of the liberalization of the attitudes and values the student brings with him when he enters college. A study by Newcomb and associates (1970) compares students in a residential college program and control students at the University of Michigan. At the end of the first year, among others, there were observed changes in family independence, social conscience, cultural sophistication, and liberalism. Increases in scores on these scales by residential college students were greater than those of the controls. The authors see these changes as a heightening of qualities already present in the student at the time he enters college. They hypothesize that such accentuation of characteristics on which residential college freshmen were initially high is the result of interaction between students: "Students who are more socially oriented interact more with their environment, and when fellow students in this environment are initially higher on a dimension, those socially oriented students will change more on attitudes relevant to that dimension" (p. 158).

Rather than substantive values (measured on a one-dimensional, linear scale), this study utilizes a general quality of life experience—the relative degree of structure in which a person is accustomed to function and the degree of the situational structure in which he must function—as the interaction which engages him and which is the impetus for change. This quality is independent of the measurement of change. Although change must still be evaluated on a one-dimensional, linear scale (less complex, more complex) the interaction which is the impetus for change is based on a quality separate from those attitudes and values used to measure change. A student need not possess the quality in order to change. In fact, change is not considered, in this framework, as an increase in a quality or attitude already present, but, in fact, change is the presence of a new attribute: the capacity to act in some new way. This definition may make it possible to answer the question, "what kind of educational program is most likely to facilitate development for what kind of student?" as well as its converse, "what kind of program is least likely to facilitate development for what kind of student?" The plausibility and consistency of our observations underscore their significance as possible answers to these questions.

Considering the prevailing quality of the students' background in relation to the quality of the Experimental College, in terms of their relative degree of structure (here defined as related to having other rather than self-directed choices) suggests that the discrepancy between these environments is greater for the students from Protestant and Catholic homes. The home background in these groups provides a more rigorous and controlled atmosphere characterized by clearly defined limits. The relatively less structured and more tolerant atmosphere of the Experimental College appears to have been challenging for relatively more of these students than for those who came from homes with a more permissive life style. In the ECP they were exposed to different types of people than those with whom they were familiar and to new styles of living and new ideas about living. They found encouragement to venture out and experiment with new ideas and new behavior in an environment that supported their autonomy, inquiry, and experimentation. While discontinuity in the environment may have produced anxiety, it stimulated new adaptive responses. There seems little question that these students felt pressed to produce and elaborate such responses. It may be that the stability of their background provided them with the integrity to experience the anxiety associated with such pressure without either reverting to earlier ways of behaving or becoming immobilized.

For students coming from homes with a less controlled atmosphere, the laissez-faire structure of the ECP was a familiar experience—both in style of life and in types of people encountered. The permissiveness of the teachers who urged the students to be autonomous (while still privately expecting them to do the "right thing") may have been reminiscent of attitudes of their own parents. Thus, they would experience less challenge in the Experimental College Program, fewer *new* responses being required of them. Apparently the more structured atmosphere of the scheduled requirements in the lower division program represented a challenge for most of these students. To have limited choice, to be scheduled, to conform to a variety of requirements in order to keep their place in school seemed to represent a challenge that demanded some new patterns of behavior from them. (Although these students encountered a similar structure while in primary and secondary school, its effect undoubtedly was heightened by the necessity of maintaining their place in college on the basis of their performance.) The relatively greater frequency of development among the students in that setting suggests such a view. It also implies that, at least at some times and for some individuals, there is something salutary about having to do something that is required.

I pointed out in an earlier chapter that students tended to choose the college setting which was most compatible with their previous experience. Yet the students who entered the unfamiliar atmosphere—either by choice or by accident—seem to have benefited specifically from its unfamiliarity. Does this finding suggest that all students from similar backgrounds might be predicted to benefit in a similar way from the Experimental Program? I cannot say. I can say, however, that the students with such a background who applied to but were not admitted to the program were classified at the same relatively low frequency as "developed" as were their counterparts (from the same background) who had not applied to the Experimental Program. Apparently the wish to enter the program was not as important to development as was the experienced discrepancy of the atmosphere, which called for new ways of functioning.

For some, the discrepancy apparently was too great. I have pointed out (in the chapter on self-selection) that some students left the program by the end of the first semester, stating that the program was too unstructured for them. These students tended to be among those who initially scored relatively low on complexity of development. However, others who scored equally low remained in the program and were among those who apparently benefited from it. What, then, is the difference between those who left and those who stayed? Those who continued may have had a greater readiness to participate in new events and respond in new ways. On the other hand, a relationship with one of the faculty may have provided a context which made such participation more possible. Clearly there are other aspects of the student's personality and of the situation that must be taken into account to understand these interactions more fully.

Much consideration currently is being given to the idea that students should have more choice in determining the shape of their education. Efforts to implement this idea include more electives and courses with pass-no pass reporting. Some institutions are considering the elimination of all breadth requirements. Others are considering the elimination of the defined major with its basic required courses. Some advocates of greater choice go so far as to propose a cafeteria model for the college, suggesting that it should set out a wide range of intellectual offerings from which students may choose without restriction.

Observations of the effect of challenge have bearing on these questions. The general thesis advanced by these observations is that a factor of major importance in the development of the student is the interaction between the student and the educational structure;

that similarity between student and structure tends to minimize the effect of the interaction whereas differences tend to maximize it. If the interaction entails challenge to the student, requiring new adaptive behavior, regardless of other changes that may occur he will tend to change in the direction of more personal complexity and functional flexibility. In the same vein, a program that offers little or no challenge is unlikely to contribute to the student's development.

The most provocative question is that of whether students are able, themselves, to choose the "right" structure—that is, the one that will be most useful to their development. Although students today typically think a great deal about change and development, it seems unlikely that many of them think of themselves in the terms of broad, general ideas of development such as I have been discussing. Since the college is organized and defined in terms of intellectual areas, fields of study, and social possibilities, these are more likely to be the students' frames of reference in making choices when planning for their education.

There is yet another consideration: if we were able to set up an educational program that utilizes the concept of adaptation to challenge, and the student were to be aware of this and "choose to be challenged," would the experience be the same as it is when the challenge is encountered unexpectedly and by chance? We know that when individuals in psychotherapy focus on the idea of changing themselves rather than on the task of self-examination, the resulting self-consciousness may become, ironically, a major obstacle to personality change. Desirable (and desired) change seems to emerge almost organically in the course of involvement in the task of self-examination; the person who is self-consciously attempting to change has difficulty engaging in that task productively. In this study we came to know individual students who avowed an intent to change themselves in college and who seemed to experience similar obstacles.

My own thinking now places me in a position which urges neither completely free choice for students—the cafeteria model—nor a completely predetermined college program. The fact is that the young men and women who come to college comprise a diverse group, representing a broad range of developmental needs. A single situation that would provide challenge for all of them would be impossible to produce in a large university setting. The best opportunity we have to challenge a broad range of students is to offer a broad range of programs, some of which are required and some of which are not. In that way we and they will collaborate in maximizing the possibility that each one will encounter a situation of salutary challenge.

Chapter 7

Personality
Development
and Cultural Change

$\mathcal{T}$he simplest model for evaluating the effectiveness of teaching is one that is similar to a standard research model. The teacher assumes a relative lack of competence in his students at the level and in the substantive area of instruction, and he assumes a readiness on the part of the students to learn. He introduces his subject matter in a way that he feels will be effective in maintaining a high level of student involvement. For evaluating the change he is attempting to effect, he uses an indicator or set of indicators such as a series of quizzes, a final examination, a term paper, or a project. In short, he has a change object (the student), a change agent (the teacher), and a method for evaluating change.

A similar array is found among the methodological tools used by psychologists engaged in empirical studies of the personal development of students in college. The study described in this book, which began with a quite systematic design, is an example. The design includes two groups of students, two educational atmospheres presumed to stimulate development in different ways or to a different degree, and a set of personality scales for measuring the anticipated change.

Occasionally a teacher is aware of qualitative changes in the behavior of the students coming to his classroom. If he has been teaching for a period of years, he may have a sense of characteristic attitudinal qualities of students which enable him to make generalized statements such as "students nowadays are conforming, docile, interested in their own pleasure and security rather than in any social questions or political problems." The latter qualities especially were so prominent in the student population of the 1950's as to lead to the term "privatism" (Reisman, 1960). By comparison, some predominant characteristics of the students in the late 1960's led to their being described by the term "activists." (The general qualities of students observed vary also according to teacher's and educator's interests. The principal of a San Francisco Bay Area high school once observed that during his fifteen years tenure entering classes changed [at observable but unpredictable intervals of time] along a dimension of organized purposefulness: students, as a corpus, he stated, were typically organized and purposeful in attitude but, inexplicably and periodically, a class would tend to disorganization, with the result that the entire student body would experience disruption characterized by discipline problems and poor academic performance during the entire four years the problem class was progressing through the school.)

A teacher with a developmental point of view begins his work with an effort to learn about his student: where he is in his general development both as a person and as a student and what is the level of his knowledge and understanding of the particular subject. The teacher who is in a position to be aware of patterns of change in students entering the school situation is in a better position to understand the individual student, and, therefore, he is able to meet him with a challenge appropriate to his level of readiness.

The psychologist studying personality development in college also is interested in observing other factors relating to the student's development besides those that are obvious, such as the curriculum and the educational structure. In these studies changes taking place in students are considered related to many different factors. One such factor, which is stressed by Sanford (1966), is the attitudinal and personality organization already achieved by the student at the time of his entrance into college. This factor may determine if he is open to change, the areas in which change is most likely, and the extent of change possible. The evaluations presented in the previous chapter serve as a case in point. In one instance, the level of complexity of the students' development, taken as a group, is related to their choice between the Experimental Program and the regular program. In the other instance, the kind of development experienced in the parental families is related to the kind of college experience that will represent a challenge to which the student must respond by developing new adaptations.

The most thoroughly investigated determinant of personality change in students is the atmosphere of the college community (Sanford, 1962c). This includes the academic atmosphere of the college as well as the social climate or the peer group culture. The effect of the college atmosphere sometimes is confounded with the effect of chronological aging or maturation of the student. Trent and Medsker (1968) were able to differentiate between these two factors by comparing changes in college students and in individuals, in the same period of life, who were working rather than going to school. The college students changed in the direction of greater independence, flexibility in functioning, freedom from opinionated thinking, and greater interest in ideas, whereas the noncollege population either did not change or changed in the opposite direction. (It must be kept in mind that a "change in the opposite direction" reflects the fact that a linear scale is being used, and it is only possible to go up or down on that scale.)

A different point of view, presented by Plant (1965), is that changes in students are related to a developmental process and do not necessarily reflect interaction with the college atmosphere. His observations suggest that change in students is independent of length of college attendance.

In the decade of the 1960s I was engaged in studying personality change during the college years. At that time I observed the increasing sophistication of students entering the University of California, Berkeley. For many years the term "freshman" carried with it the image of a shy young person inclined to cling to conventional forms in social dealings, to admire and respect persons in positions of authority, and to identfy with those older than himself. Many freshmen of this "old-fashioned" variety still exist. However, in my observation, beginning students appeared increasingly self-confident and more independent of authority and conventions. They were more aware of world events and problems and were eager to contribute ideas for their solution. Such student qualities were reported in the press later in the decade in connection with student activism, but it has been assumed that they characterized only a small minority of students. Our study suggested that these qualities are increasingly characteristic of freshmen. Those whom we studied on entrance in 1965 differed in many respects from the freshmen of four years earlier, and the nature of these differences suggests further factors contributing to personality changes in young people. These findings are of interest because they raise fundamental questions about the study of student development and about current orientation of college teaching and academic structures.

Katz tested freshmen in 1961 and retested them in 1965, administering a questionnaire that included the Authoritarianism and Ethnocentrism scales and a number of scales from the Omnibus Personality Inventory (Katz and associates, 1968). He reported that the 1961 freshmen made significant changes when they responded to the same inventory in 1965. He summarizes these changes as reflecting a movement toward greater open-mindedness, tolerance, flexibility, and realistic thinking. Stereotyped views of right and wrong appear to have given way to a broader acceptance of human diversity and to a more humanized conscience. Instead of their earlier inhibition, the scores reflect a tendency to express impulses and emotions, to act rebelliously, and to have an increased awareness and appreciation of aesthetic experiences.

For the most part, our 1965 freshmen could be described in similar terms. All but two of the scale scores of the students entering in 1965 differed significantly from those of the 1961 freshmen and were either essentially the same as those of the graduating seniors or even more extreme in the direction of the changes made by the seniors. This pattern holds for both men and women in the 1965 freshman group. The two scales that do not follow this pattern are the Masculinity and Schizoid Functioning Scales. Schizoid Functioning scores decreased during their four years of college, whereas the 1965 male freshmen scores were as high as those of the 1961 freshmen, and those scores of the female freshmen in 1965 were significantly higher than those of the 1961 female freshmen. This suggests that the greater psychological freedom of the 1965 freshmen may be accompanied by feelings of isolation, alienation, disorientation, and identity diffusion. The scores also may reflect, in part, an attitude of greater freedom to express such feelings on the part of the 1965 freshmen.

Katz also reported percentages of "yes" answers by Berkeley male students to some of the items in the questionnaire. Comparison with responses of 1965 freshmen students suggests a continuing shift of opinions. Table 2 (following page) shows that more of the 1965 freshmen had high intellectual and artistic interests (items 1–4) and endorsed statements of independence (items 5–7); fewer were inclined to check items suggesting conventional behavior (items 8–10), or Puritan morality and blind respect for authority and patriotism (items 11–15); fewer subscribed to items supporting the ideas of order, certainty and religion (items 16–18); and more seemed attuned to a relativistic outlook (items 19–20) than did the 1961 freshmen or even the 1965 seniors.

The fact that 1965 seniors and freshmen have similar scores, reflecting similar attitudes in most dimensions, suggests a common influence. Three conditions of personality change during college years were described earlier in this chapter: the personality organization at the time of entrance into college, the atmosphere of the college community, and a developmental process relatively independent of the other two conditions. It seems unlikely that these conditions of change could provide the common influence producing the sort of similarity of attitudes that has been described. The two

Table 2

PERCENTAGE OF YES RESPONSES AMONG 1961 FRESHMEN,
1965 SENIORS, AND 1965 FRESHMEN

	1961 Freshmen	1965 Seniors	1965 Freshmen
1. I enjoy reading essays on serious or philosophical subjects.	54	58	66
2. I like to read about artistic or literary achievements.	37	44	54
3. I have spent a lot of time listening to serious music.	37	42	47
4. Trends toward abstractionism and the distortion of reality have corrupted much art in recent years.	41	25	20
5. At times I have very much wanted to leave home.	53	61	68
6. I have often either broken rules (school, club, and so on) or inwardly rebelled against them.	38	42	50
7. My home life was always happy.	53	47	31
8. I do not like to see people carelessly dressed.	58	48	41
9. I dislike women who disregard the usual social or moral conventions.	46	24	25
10. I prefer people who are never profane.	31	17	18
11. What youth needs most is strict discipline, rugged determination, and the will to work and fight for family and country.	53	22	21

Table 2 (Cont.)

PERCENTAGE OF YES RESPONSES AMONG 1961 FRESHMEN,
1965 SENIORS, AND 1965 FRESHMEN

	1961 Freshmen	1965 Seniors	1965 Freshmen
12. More than anything else, it is good hard work that makes life worthwhile.	52	36	26
13. The surest way to a peaceful world is to improve people's morals.	37	25	26
14. In the final analysis parents turn out to be right about things.	79	53	53
15. We should respect the work of our forefathers and not think that we know better than they did.	40	19	16
16. I don't like to work on a problem unless there is the possibility of coming out with a clear-cut and unambiguous answer.	42	28	22
17. In religious matters I believe I would have to be called a skeptic or an agnostic.	40	62	65
18. God hears our prayers.	64	38	39
19. Moral codes are relevant only when they fit the specific situations; if the situations differ, they are merely abstract irrelevancies.	49	57	59
20. The only meaning to existence is the one which man gives himself.	70	78	78

groups of students are a different age, they have been exposed to different sorts of school and social experiences, and they are at different developmental stages. However, the nature of the attitudes shared by them suggests that a common influence could be the social revolution widely assumed to be taking place throughout the world, especially in the younger generation.

The existence of such a revolution is indicated by such empirical observations as youth demanding a voice in decision-making, insisting on emancipation from authority, demonstrating for rights. One may consider such protests as arising from early childhood experiences; these two groups of middle-class Americans were exposed to the post-World War II child-rearing practices which stressed consideration of the child's wishes and of his autonomy and need for self-determination. On the other hand, one may consider the revolution to be related to aspects of general social change brought about by rapid technological growth. The latter often involves the recognition (by minority groups as well as youth in general) of the disparity between ideals and practice and between the haves and the have-nots. One may understand the revolution in terms of all of these factors working together and of others as well.

The important consideration is that youth is changing, especially in social outlook and attitudes and in interpersonal style. In part it may reflect the young people's response to their experiences in the world as they perceive it. In part it may be the younger youth emulating the older youth, taking on their styles and attitudes. Our interviews with students during their four years in college suggest that both kinds of influence are important. Thus, the mean scale scores of the two groups, presented earlier, can be seen as reflecting in part strongly and genuinely held attitudes and in part attitudes that are important to express because they are regarded as the hallmark of youth. Goffman (1959) refers to these as "presentational" attitudes used in "staging a character." Young people of all ages are exposed to attitudes, and to the events contributing to the development of the attitudes, through mass communication made possible by modern technology. The whole process of change obviously is accelerated by such exposure.

Are we to conclude, then, that the scores of the 1965 freshmen represent the same level of development as do the similar scores of the seniors? (By development, I mean the development of the total personality.) Probably the 1965 freshmen are in some respects more complex in their overall personality development than are the 1961 freshmen; because of living in a highly technological society they have been exposed more often to complex events and have had to respond to more experiences of those events than did the 1961 freshmen at the same age. However, it is important to recognize that they have had little time to integrate much of this experience into the total functioning of their personalities. In this sense they are not as well developed as are the seniors, who have had time and opportunity, on their own, with peers or with teachers, to review and in some cases to act in terms of, and to integrate some of their major experiences. (Dewey, 1958, held that human organisms vary in richness, depending on the particular history of each. The variation is not simply a matter of "more" or "less" experience but, rather, it is a matter of what Dewey called doing and undergoing: that is, the organism must achieve a balance between acting and experiencing, between being a locus of causality and a locus of perception. To put it another way, the person must both experience and act in terms of that experience in order to be richer in meanings.) Our students' higher freshmen scores on the Schizoid Functioning Scale would suggest a lack of integration and a greater sense of alienation on the part of the students in the 1965 entering class.

The possibility of accelerating development and of changes in attitudes and outlook on the part of succeeding generations of young people must be taken into account in studies of personality change and in studies of change during college particularly. (The interval between generations would appear to be growing shorter, if not biologically, then certainly in terms of changes in attitudes and values. The observations under discussion suggest that a new generation of college students appears every four to six years.) In attempting to understand what sorts of experiences during the college years are dynamically related to changes taking place, it seems important to take into account the fact that, as Marshall McLuhan (1967) observes, the whole world is a village. In technological societies everyone can be aware almost simultaneously of events occurring throughout the world, often while they are happening. Our perception of students' experiences must be expanded to include not only what is happening on the campus but what also is happening in the outside world. We need, moreover, to devise

methods for describing and evaluating development that will take
into account other aspects of total personality functioning. Some
aspects of personality functioning, such as complexity, attitudes
toward authority and independence of thinking, and attitudes regarding expression of feelings, can be evaluated by means of the
scales used in this study. More subtle changes in such qualities as
the extent and depth of engagement in interpersonal relationships,
in the maturity of long-range interests, and in integration of experience are more difficult to evaluate. One might expect the 1965
seniors to differ from the freshmen in such personality qualities.

Other considerations also are important. During the period
in question, 1961 to 1965, Berkeley became recognized as one of the
world centers for the youthful revolution and attracted a large number, probably a disproportionately large number, of young people
characterized by the attitudes represented in the scores reported
here. This factor could, in itself, account for the fact that 1965
freshmen scores apparently represent a higher level of development
on the part of many freshmen students as compared with those who
entered University of California, Berkeley, in previous years. In
other words, the findings may reflect, to some extent, a particular
quality of the Berkeley campus in the period of the mid-1960s.

It is more likely that this was an early expression of a continuing trend on American campuses. Students with the characteristics just described are now, in the decade of the 1970s, becoming
more in evidence on American campuses that have been traditionally sheltered and where student attitudes have been traditionally conservative. Many of these smaller colleges are located at a
distance from major population centers such as the San Francisco
Bay Area, where because of the coming together of many diverse
social elements social change tends to accelerate. In short, I am
suggesting that the student characteristics that emerged so dramati-
ically at Berkeley in the mid 1960's were harbingers of student
characteristics that are becoming generally prevalent in colleges
and universities throughout the nation. Similar student qualities
and an accompanying unrest also are reported emerging on Euro-
pean campuses today.

Given the facts of self-selection (Chapter Three), the characteristics and behavior of students in the Experimental College

Program may predict characteristics of students entering special programs being initiated in many colleges and universities. This probably is true of students choosing the cluster college and special programs that foster the development of a community of students and faculty. Although it was not a residential college, the Experimental College Program was, in many respects, a forerunner of the burgeoning cluster college movement.

Finally, there are implications that can be drawn from these observations that are pertinent to the profession of teaching in any academic structure. When the Social Maturity and the Impulse Expression scales were developed, it seemed important that the college consider how to open up the shy, inhibited freshman to help him recognize the importance of feelings and impulses and to consider them when making decisions. It now appears, at least on many campuses, that educators might better consider the opposite question: if students already are accustomed to act on impulse and to act independently when they arrive in college, how can they be helped to learn to postpone action in the interest of carrying tasks through to satisfactory conclusion?

Another perspective of the same matter is suggested by Chickering: "It is to foster increased differentiation that a liberal arts college aims to free an individual from the limitations of outlook brought from his own locale, his family, his social class, and his national heritage" (1971, p. 292). In the past, much of the liberating process has been the result of student exposure to a broader range of information and consideration of points of view different than those to which he was accustomed. Today, the liberating process must include increased emphasis on learning how to analyze and evaluate the bewildering array of experiences to which the student is exposed by the very fact of being alive in the contemporary world.

Chapter 8

Research
Psychologists
Change Too

*T*he uniformity of research pub-
lished in our psychological journals always has seemed to me cur-
iously unnatural. Article after article in journal after journal is
written according to a predictable formula: a hypothesis, a more or
less empirical test of the hypothesis, and the results of the test usually
with a few brief, highly qualified statements about some general
implications of the findings. Rarely does the researcher say anything
to suggest that he was wrong or, more to the point, that he has
changed his views of the matter under study as a result of his in-

92

vestigation. If the old dictum that we learn by doing is valid, then something more must be happening to psychologists who are doing research than is reported in the literature.

I am a psychologist who, for some years, has been practicing a kind of psychotherapy that attempts to investigate, rather than to shape, the individual. The intention of such investigation is to help the individual in his efforts to understand his difficulty in living, so that he might, if he wishes, change his ways. In the course of such investigation I often have the experience of finding that as my patient is changing his view of things, so, also, am I, and that I, as well as he, come to a very different concept of one or another aspect of human life. (And, where the educational structure permits teacher-student interaction, teachers often find themselves changing in similar fashion.) I experienced a similar effect—a new perspective in my own thinking—in carrying out the formal research here reported. I had no reason to anticipate any change in myself. My academic preparation for doing psychological research had not led me to such an expectation. Furthermore, I did not make the connection between investigation in the psychotherapy office and in the research office, and it therefore came as a surprise when, in the process of my research, I became aware of a change in my views relative to the subject under study and also to the method in which I had set out to study it.

Both the clinical and the research experiences focused questions for me about the nature of psychological research. Particularly, why does psychological research—which is, after all, considered one of the "life sciences" and which addresses itself to questions about living—so often seem totally removed from life? My answer is that psychologists too infrequently acknowledge error and change in ourselves, both in our concept of what we are studying and of how we are studying it. Too often we are inclined to cling to our theory, our concepts, and especially our research method, despite repeated evidence that it is not working. I am suggesting that psychological research has little to say about the problems of living today because we too often refuse to acknowledge that we are wrong in our methods of study.

This study of the Experimental College Program was

planned as a systematic, empirical research. Comparisons in development of students in two different educational settings were to be evaluated. The research design included the specification of the two educational settings, an experimental and two control groups, and quantitative measures of development which were to be applied at the beginning, middle, and end of the four-year period in which the study was carried out. In short, the design of the study had the requisites of sound scientific research—controlled conditions and objective measurements applied systematically so as to make possible replication of the research.

My experience in executing the plan of the study was a reversal of Alice's experience in Wonderland when she finds herself running and running, with the landscape whizzing by, and in spite of the furious activity she eventually realizes that she has not budged.

In doing the research I, unlike Alice, believed myself to be standing still, and it was from this presumably immobile position that I was attempting a careful measurement of the students' developmental changes by means of controls and precise comparisons. However, the experience became one in which everything, including the students and myself as well was in a state of constant change.

For one thing, my reliance on the research design began to change. The design of the study implied that, since the educational atmospheres were different, development of students in them could be expected to be different. Efforts to measure those differences produced equivocal results: for example, although students might have begun at different levels of development, by the end of two years the differences became insignificant (Chapter Five). Even when differences in development at the outset were controlled, the results were still equivocal: groups defined as different in terms of their initial level of development showed no difference in development in either of the two educational conditions. It would have been logical to conclude that there was, in fact, no difference in development in the two atmospheres.

A redefinition of student characteristics—one taking into account an important quality (that is, degree of structure) in which the two atmospheres differ and with which student qualities might be expected to interact—showed significant differences in development in different groups of students in the two atmospheres (Chapter Six). The original concept of the study seemed vindicated.

It was brought home to me, however, that the original concept easily could lead to a way of thinking that might oversimplify all factors under study. Comparison of groups undergoing different conditions yields information about an average tendency in the group or an average effect of the condition, which may say little or nothing about the individual. I would like to note here that Chickering (1971, p. 309) states, "Studies of significant subgroups may often reveal change and impact not apparent when total populations are examined." It seems important to acknowledge also that the study of individuals may reveal phenomena not apparent when significant subgroups are examined.

Soon after the students responded to our questionnaire at the end of their second year it became evident that individuals in the different groups were varying widely from the group means. Some students who had started out with a high degree of self-sufficiency and independence of judgment appeared to be changing, according to our scales, in the direction of more authoritarian attitudes, in fact to dependence on absolute authority. Moreover, this happened in a program expected to foster a diametrically opposite development. On the other hand, in the regular program which was presumed to be rigid, stultifying development by its impersonality and lack of freedom—some students were making observable developmental change in the direction of greater personal freedom and autonomy. This was, in some degree, expected; the measure of a central tendency is based on and represents diverse responses of individuals in the group. However, such variation underscored the fact that the differences in group means, although statistically significant, had little to do with what actually was happening to individual students in college.

The interviews, focused on the individual students' experiences, showed even more clearly that what was happening was a very different, more varied story than the group measures possibly could indicate. Despite some obvious uniformities, both the experimental and the control conditions were being experienced very differently by different students in each of them. It gradually became evident that the original idea—to compare the usual undergraduate program with the special program—was too simple. Neither program provided the unitary experience that the research design assumed. The conventional program was not the monolithic machine it had been assumed to be. Students were, within it, creating programs for themselves that were just as imaginative and relevant as the special program conceived by the faculty of the Experimental College Program. Contrary to popular opinion, some students not only had time to think but were able to do so even while carrying extra courses in order to complete degree requirements at an accelerated rate. (It was my opinion, too, that the courses making up the undergraduate education at Berkeley at that time were so crowded with material and so demanding of the students' time that the experience was, as one student put it, "like trying to take a drink out of a fire hose.") Similarly, the special program was far from its goal of providing the sort of unitary experience implied in the research design. Despite fundamental agreement about the nature of the program, it turned out that the five members of the faculty had different perceptions of their roles; similarly, among the 150 students there were many (possibly 150) different ways of relating to the program. The design overlooked the fact that the student has much to do with the way a given educational program is perceived, experienced, and used. It set aside the fact that experience is not unitary and that the educational experience is a particularly complex one. My view is substantiated by another. Chickering states: "The impact of a class, course, or curriculum, of a teacher, peer or culture, will vary with the backgrounds, ability levels, and personality characteristics of the students. But higher education has given little attention to this obvious principle. Instead, students have been treated as though they were billiard balls, all alike in shape, size, and density, all stationary till struck." Psychological research method of the sort I started out to do also has given little attention to this fact.

An awareness of a changing view of students also began to develop for me. I, for one, began the study with special interest in the "turned on" student: a student who appeared relatively free to make use of his own resources, especially his imagination, one who seemed unusually curious, eager to seek out varied experiences, and easily able to verbalize his thought and feelings. But, as the first two years of the study went by, there was a growing sense of disappointment occasioned by the all-too-obvious fact that students who had been regarded as representatives of the "turned on" type—students who had been imagined to be unusual and full of promise—were, in actuality, not going anywhere. It had to be acknowledged that, developmentally, they had made little progress. On the other hand, some of the "straight" students much more conventional in outlook, much less "promising" were seriously engaged and noticeably changing. They were thinking about matters relevant to their life, they were arranging their academic programs to facilitate that thinking, they were pursuing their intentions consistently, and, more important, to completion. They were not simply "turned on"—they were *going* somewhere.

A related change in our view of students was the realization that students' complaints about college irrelevance, impersonality, inflexibility—were, at least in part, symptomatic of the times. These were the subjects about which it was fashionable to complain, and the manner of complaint also was prescribed and, as time revealed, wearisomely predictable.

A similar observation changed our view of change. It became evident that "change" had a priority in student ideology. It was considered a mark of success to change while in college, and, therefore, it was fashionable to change. There are, therefore, students who change—according to fashion—furiously, and often; these are the ones who remain, basically, the same in fundamental attitudes and values (see Chapter Ten). For the same reason, it also became apparent that the response to attitude and opinion scales now was different, that there now was a self-consciousness that altered the meaning of the response as compared with the period when the scales first were developed. Responses to items about racial intolerance are the most obvious: "tolerance" now is an ideology; it no longer is a simple expression of basic personality disposition. Thus, changes in scores on personality measures could not be taken to represent changes in personality, as anticipated when the study began. Fifteen years had intervened between the original construction of the scale and our use of it, and during those years tolerance became a conscious ideology. Compelling evidence was presented by students who scored very low on measures of intolerance of racial minorities but at the same time expressed extreme intolerance of military men, government officials, college administrators, and other members of "the establishment".

This phenomenon of "response set" (an individual's attitude about the items he is answering in a questionnaire, especially how he feels he should answer them) is a factor commonly associated with the use of questionnaires. It is customary to take steps to control, or to minimize, or to eliminate the effects of response set either by means of the instructions given the person taking the questionnaire, or by measuring the degree of the "set" and quantitatively discounting the effects it may have on the person's true response.

Our observation was that response set was not an error to be eliminated in evaluating students' responses to questionnaires, but it was rather an integral part of the phenomenon we were studying. It is part of the complexity of the personality change taking place in college students that, in addition to their basic attitudes and values, they also hold attitudes about what attitudes and values should be held by the sort of person they want to think of themselves as being or becoming.

It became apparent that cues for this complex of attitudes come from many sources. We gradually realized that all of our students, regardless of their experiences in college, were experiencing and responding to very compelling world events. Such experiences and responses were contributing in a major way to changes in their attitudes. Our concept of their life-space as contained in one or another academic program on the college campus was far too limited.

All of these observations gradually emerged into our awareness as the study progressed, and they led to changes not only in our thinking about research but also in the execution of this particular study. For example, just as the study had begun with a traditional style of design, the first interviews also were of a traditional design: an interview schedule, carefully prepared in advance, required an interviewer to ask specific questions in a way that would minimize his effect on student responses. The student was given an opportunity to discuss his own concerns, but this opportunity was afforded him only after we explored the series of topics which we, the researchers, believed to be representative. I realized that our very efforts at objectivity, at minimizing our effect on the student's responses, were affecting those responses most profoundly. As a result, our interviews were changed to a more naturalistic sort. (The term "naturalistic" is used to distinguish inquiry into phenomena in their natural state from inquiry by means of manipulation of variables and conditions in a controlled experimental setting. We chose to adopt this manner of interviewing because it was more appropriate to the questions we were investigating, namely, the nature of the experience of the students. In making this change in method, I was aware that in the social sciences the prevailing attitude holds naturalistic research to be a second-class method. As Willems and Raush state, "there is still the tendency . . . to view naturalistic research as a preliminary, early-stage, or even bird-watching, type of activity" (1969, p. 8). Nevertheless, the change proved to be liberating to the interviewers and productive of many new observations.)

Although we carefully reviewed our knowledge and observations of college life and of the particular student we were about to interview, and although we formulated what we thought were important questions regarding the particular student to be interviewed, we kept these questions in the back of our minds and deliberately refrained from asking them. Instead, we encouraged the student to talk about whatever was currently engaging his interest. At the same time, rather than avoiding our effect on the interview, we often went out of our way to produce an effect. By stating our own views on a matter under discussion, we often could observe the way in which the student might react to a different point of view, to an observation about himself which he had not considered, or simply to the interest of a participant observer of a different age and generation. The researcher is, after all, a participant in the process, and, like the psychotherapist, he cannot, in fact, separate himself from it and be objective.

As the end of the study was nearing, our original questions and some of our means of generating answers seemed anachronistic and inappropriate. Instead of the final assessment that was planned (another administration of the personality scales), we attempted to engage the students in a spontaneous assessment of their own. The students were asked to come in to discuss the study with us. Discussions were held in groups of from four to six students meeting with a member of the research staff. The groups were made up according to available time of the students and therefore included students from any of the three research groups, mixed more or less randomly. The three groups included: 1) the students who volunteered and were selected to participate in the Experimental College Program, 2) those who volunteered and were not included by the random selection, and, 3) those who did not volunteer. These discussion groups also brought together students who had different degrees of participation in the study. Some had responded to our initial questionnaire as entering freshmen; they had not been available at the time of the second testing and hence were unfamiliar with the study. A majority had responded to both the initial questionnaire and the one at the end of the second year. Some, in addition to the two questionnaires, had been interviewed once each semester and were quite familiar with the study and its purposes. At the beginning of the ninety-minute meeting the students were asked to state their participation in the study and their understanding of what it was about. After it became clear to all what the general purpose and format of the study had been, the students present were asked to write their predictions of the results of the study. The remaining time was devoted to the discussion that emerged. The discussions were taped for later and more careful study. We now saw the students not only as passive subjects of our study but as active participants, and, therefore, we made another change. We paid them for their time in the meetings.

This change in the final assessment was not undertaken lightly. It violates the pattern of the research design; it makes impossible a before-and-after four-year comparison in terms of the same measures. It might have been simpler to conclude the study as was originally intended and to plan to change any future studies undertaken. However, in terms of the changes that took place within us as a result of our research observations, we felt that it would have been senseless to repeat those measures: first, because we realized that the original concept of two different conditions was too simple. Taken in the final analysis, there are as many Universities of California, Berkeley, as there are students in it; and even the individual perception of the university, or of any program within it, changes over time. Also, it would not make sense because we knew many of our measures often evoked responses in terms of conscious ideology and not fundamental personality disposition. Most important is our impression—from observing individual students in interviews and ourselves, for that matter, in the process of this study that change does not take place in a linear form, as the use of the before-after measures assumes. Change seems to appear more nearly in a circular or spiral form, which, in the linear perspective, may be seen as an ebb and flow with, sometimes in the long run, an overall progression. And finally, it seems doubtful that the changes we observed in students can be related easily to educational structure; that is, the structure is too diffuse, and there are too many other events important in the students' lives that overlap with educational experiences.

In brief, the impact of the study on those of us doing it was to make us seriously question our instruments. We started with a concept of change and ended questioning the validity of the concept itself, questioning whether it is possible to measure change in any meaningful way or if it is possible to measure the relationship between change and a particular educational experience. These questions became so compelling that they led to a redefinition of our concepts and a new approach to observation. Our new task, of evaluating our discussions with the students, was not easy. But at least it made sense to be doing it.

Sir Peter Medawar, Nobel research biologist, said, "Good scientific method must provide for the origin and prevalence of error; a good deal of a scientist's time is spent in being mistaken" (1966–1967). Clearly this applies to research psychologists as well. It is by recognizing our mistakes that we may make the process of investigation more fruitful.

Chapter 9

Personalization
of the Educational
Experience

The gradual changes in our method and questions brought us closer to an appreciation of the real-life experiences students were having in college. In the second two years our interest, and the study along with it, shifted from an original focus on quantitative differences in developmental changes to consideration of the quality of student experiences. We did not completely forego using quantitative measures, but we devoted much more attention to what was happening to each student whom we came to know. From that observational level, it became possible

to see the variety of experiences that college can offer. By understanding the personal experiences of students we hoped to learn
considerably more about their developmental changes. Because the
Experimental College Program was defined in terms of the "development of human understanding," and according to Tussman,
"to fit us for the life of active membership in the democratic community" (1969, pp. 3–4), or the goals of liberal education, it is
of particular interest to discover experiences that further such
goals: how does a student develop a full appreciation of himself as
an individual in relationship with others and as a member of a
community in which he has responsibility for others? While such
questions were not explicitly a part of the study, in retrospect they
emerged with increasing insistence as pertinent considerations. They
now seem appropriate questions with which to address the data.

The basic plan of the Experimental College was to provide
a curriculum—determined by the faculty and unequivocally required—which would give the student the knowledge the faculty
felt he could use as a tool in his subsequent academic and personal
life; a sufficient period of time during which the student would be
free from the pressures of premature commitment to specialization
and professionalism; an educational structure in which he could
learn to reflect, to judge, to understand—in the interest of enlightened action; and, finally, the overall process of the program was to
be facilitated by continuity derived from the fact that the same
group of students would remain in close working contact with the
same faculty for a period of two years.

There is a major advantage in such an arrangement because
it permits the student—in all his unique individuality—to be revealed to the teacher. The teacher can learn to know and respond
to the student as an individual and encourage him in the development of basic skills, academic knowledge, and personal growth.
Such a relationship did develop, in fact, for many individual students in association with individual faculty members. The promise
of earthly paradise was not, however, completely realized in the end.
Because of the vicissitudes of the first trial of the program, because
of personnel changes in faculty and among the teaching assistants,
this happy association did not occur as frequently or as ideally as
was hoped. Nevertheless, many of these students did have a highly

personalized experience in their first two years of college—a rare event (if it exists at all) in the usual lower division program.

By *personalization* I mean the heightening of the experience of oneself when such experience takes place in the context of a relationship between two individuals. The earliest awareness of self emerges from a relationship with another. In like manner, I believe, it is in the context of a personal relationship that a student has the opportunity to see himself in sharp relief as a unique self—as he is closely related to his teachers and fellow students. He also is able to observe his teachers at close range and to see them for what they are: not as idealized superiors but as fellow humans with ideals sometimes imperfectly realized. In that context, the student's sense of himself and of his relationship to his education and to other people can become clearer, and his actions can become more a matter of personal choice.

There were two aspects to the quality of personal experience in the ECP: first, the students' sense of being special because of their membership in the ECP, and, more important, their long and close personal association with the faculty and, during the first year, with the teaching assistants.

We had wondered whether there would be a hothouse atmosphere about the Experimental College. For example, would the group of students be identified as "special" by the rest of the college community? Would they, in that case, come to think of themselves as an elite group? During the time the program was in progress nothing apparently suggested that the students were held in such special regard by other students. Among themselves, however, there were some who held themselves as group members deserving of special esteem. The matter was not frequently or spontaneously discussed, however, which may have been because they accepted it as a matter of course that theirs was an elite group.

In the group discussion at the end of the fourth year, students in the regular college program made it clear that they were very much aware of the special status of the Experimental College Program students whom they had encountered. Awareness usually focused on the notion of relative work load: the ECP student was perceived as being subject to much freedom and little demand. It was believed, for example, that he could take the time to read a book intensively—over several weeks if he felt the need or inclination—or that he had ample time to write papers or to engage in other student activities. On the other hand, the student in the regular program saw himself as an individual sorely pressed—reading books and writing papers simultaneously without adequate time to give justice to either—as he struggled to prepare for quizzes and examinations. Time was the main factor about which envy centered. Often regular program students did not know, personally, any of the ECP students, but they felt they knew, by hearsay, the academic luxury those fortunate academic peers were experiencing.

Obviously, Experimental College Program students were seen as a group set apart. It is impossible to believe that the students themselves did not have a sense of special and privileged status. Indeed, some students were overtly aware of special distinction: as a mark of proud identity they appeared in sweatshirts clearly emblazoned: *Joe's College.*

There were other signs that pointed to them as a special group. For one thing, it was obvious that they, as a group, were being studied. During group discussions at the end of the fourth year, students from both college programs expressed the idea that the study was of the "Tussman College." The focus of interest, in short, was felt to be on the Experimental College students and not on the students scattered through the rest of the University.

During the first year of the Experimental College Program, Harvey, the participant observer for the study, attended the weekly meetings and discussions, which included all students and all faculty members. He regularly sat in on the seminars, participated in the informal evening programs, and met with the faculty in most of their regular meetings. In the process, he became personally acquainted with many students. He continued his participation throughout the second year, although less frequently. Because he was regularly in evidence, he was a person of high visibility to the students. Because he also was identified as the director of the Psychiatric Department of the Student Health Service, the students were naturally curious about him and his function in their program. Although they identified him as a consultant for the faculty rather than as a participant observer for the study, his interest in the students was obvious, and many responded to him in kind. By some he was regarded as resident psychiatrist to the Experimental Program. To what more elevated status symbol could any group hope to aspire?

The unique opportunity the program afforded to get to know teachers on a continuous, day-to-day basis reinforced the general background of specialness. Few, if any, other undergraduates similarly were privileged. Most ECP students were in almost daily, personal contact with each other, with their faculty members, and, during the first year, with their teaching assistants. To a group of bright young freshmen, such an opportunity for intimate acquaintance with prestigious persons must have seemed attractive. Even though an individual might choose not to avail himself of the privilege, it was nevertheless there—available to him by reason of his membership in a select group of students.

More important, however, was the personalization of the overall educational experience made possible by intimate contact. In the large classes typical of major colleges and universities, students have little real opportunity to deal directly with their teachers. What experience they have with older persons in the college is usually with officials and administrators, persons perceived as dehumanized and somewhat arbitrary troubleshooters for particular problems.

To be sure, all students do not seek intimate relationships with faculty members. The faculty of institutions of higher learning are criticized for impersonality, distance, and unavailability. Such criticism may be justified, not so much on the basis of dereliction of teachers, but because of their preoccupation with career demands stressing scholarship, research, and publication. It is also true, however, that a young person, at this point in his life, usually is psychologically engaged in severing close attachments with adults —particularly those of his immediate family. Developmentally, he is in the process of relinquishing his childhood relationships. It therefore frequently occurs that professors who are intensely interested in personalized teaching and who make an effort to hold regular office hours in which to talk with their students find themselves sitting in an empty office. It may be that many students welcome the anonymity of a large class and an aloof teacher, even while they complain loudly—and perhaps fashionably—of the impersonality of both.

In the regular lower division program a student must go to some effort to make personal contact with his teachers. In the Experimental College Program the situation was reversed: a student had trouble avoiding such experiences, which were, however, observed as very meaningful to the students. Some of these observations differentiate ECP students from unadmitted volunteers for the program. Since the two groups originally were identically matched, in most respects, any subsequent difference between them seems clearly attributable to experiences in the ECP.

In the first year the students in the ECP had the opportunity to know the teaching assistants, who, like the faculty, were vital, interested, and intelligent, presenting clearly identifiable, highly visible models. In some instances they proved to be leaders, encouraging the younger students to try new ways of life that were not necessarily restricted to the academic life.

This was the period immediately following the Free Speech Movement, when new manners and methods for students were emerging. In addition to challenging the educational structure, students were engaged in changing other institutions. For example, the costuming and grooming of students was altering radically during the first year or two, and some of the teaching assistants led the way. Long hair, head bands, bare feet, beards, and the ubiquitous beads appeared among the students. There also were changes in style of living. Several teaching assistants were known to be sharing their living quarters with a student of the opposite sex—a pattern which expanded rapidly throughout the college population during the next four years. Many students participating in our study were sharing living quarters with students of the opposite sex, some with one partner, some with a mixed group. Students in both educational programs began such arrangements early, some even in their freshman year. However, by the senior year the Experimental College Program students were coeducationally cohabiting in significantly greater proportions than were students in the regular program during the first two years ($p < .01$).

Another innovation had to do with the use of drugs. When

this freshman class entered college, drug experimentation among students was beginning to accelerate. In the Experimental College Program some of the teaching assistants were actively interested in experimenting with drug-induced changes in states of consciousness. Their interest aroused the interest of the young students. This, of course, is not intended to suggest that drugs were a part of the ECP. Emphatically they were not. Just as with any interest that might engage the faculty, and especially because the teaching assistants were closer in age and more visible and available than were the faculty, the younger students heard about it, talked about it, and were engaged by it. Gossip that a son of one faculty member had been arrested for possession of drugs no doubt added another personal dimension to their interest.

In the first freshman semester, by the end of the third month, this interest had burgeoned to such a degree that some of the staff— even some of the teaching assistants who favored experimentation— became alarmed that drugs might ruin the college, if not in its actual functioning, at least in reputation. Some of the teaching assistants and student leaders proposed a secret cadre to instruct students in ways to avoid detection. The participant observer deflected this scheme into an evening meeting devoted, instead, to a discussion of drugs. In an effort to set the theme of the discussion and to express his general view of drug use, he quoted Kafka: "A person may choose not to suffer; that may be the only choice he is given to make."

The ensuing discussion ran a wild gamut ranging from such extreme ideas as, "the army is stockpiling LSD to give to the Russians so that the army can take over their country" to, "if I were mayor of Berkeley, I'd set up tables to give out LSD—our problems would disappear."

There was a wide range of individual differences among both the students and the teaching assistants. Two of the latter, for example, were very interested in drug use and—directly or by example—encouraged experimentation among the students. Three, on the other hand, were very much opposed to such activity. These were strongly supported by the program secretary, herself a recent graduate at the M.A. level and also a personal model and confidante of considerable influence with the students.

That the close personal contacts fostered in the Experimental College experience had their effect on overall attitudes is reflected in what students told us about experimenting with drugs. Toward the end of their first semester on campus we asked them, individually, about their feelings and attitudes about trying drugs; we inquired whether they had had such experiences themselves or knew of such experiences indirectly through friends or classmates. In this context a significantly larger proportion of men and women in the Experimental College than in the regular program told us they had tried LSD (18 per cent to 5 per cent) and marijuana (27 per cent to 13 per cent). Those interviewed in the regular program included the students who had volunteered for the ECP. The effect, therefore, of the close personal contact in the Experimental College is strongly underscored. Whether the difference is a real difference in actual experimentation or in the students' willingness to discuss it with us, it nevertheless reflects the effect of a greater sense of being personally related to the people in their college community.

Drugs played another role. Individual students had the experience of suddenly finding themselves outside the law and, therefore, outside their own society. (The experience of one student, who was particularly articulate about being able to look at his society from the outside, will be presented in the next chapter.)

At the social level, attitudes about drugs sometimes determined the grouping among the ECP students. Three groups formed: those who favored drug use, those who opposed it, and those who—whether they tried it or not—did not take a stand.

But the drug issue was more than one of social groupings, for at times the use of drugs became a matter of identity as well. Students use various means to differentiate themselves in general and, in particular, to differentiate themselves from parents. A year or two earlier, attitudes about the Free Speech Movement may have been used to separate students from parents. At that time drugs became the point of contention, and their use by students represented a badge of courage. A striking instance of this aspect of drug use occurred at a retreat for the students and faculty that was held at the end of the first year at a quiet place in the country. In the evening a large campfire was set ablaze, and faculty and students relaxed around it. The drug users removed themselves from this group and could be heard whooping it up off in the bushes. The others stayed around the campfire with the faculty, roasting marshmallows and, in some instances, drinking wine. When the faculty retired, the students got together and shared each other's stimulants —pot or wine. Faculty presence had an effect on the way each group stated its identity. With the faculty out of sight, they merged their efforts; both groups became more open in defining themselves in terms they knew the faculty would not approve.

The importance of the personalization of experience can be demonstrated in still another area of behavior. At the end of the fourth year a study of the records of the Student Health Service showed a consistent and marked difference in the amount of use of their services by the ECP students than by other students. The Student Health Service at Berkeley includes a variety of clinical services for registered students. During the period of this study the entire service was made up of seventeen out-patient clinics representing various medical specialties, including a department of psychiatry, an eighty-bed hospital, and a surgery. The use of all of these services was significantly greater among the Experimental College students. Thus, 11 per cent of them, as compared with 5 per cent of the other students, visited the various medical clinics more than twenty-five times during the four years ($X^2 = 5.05$, df 1, $p < .05$.)

These were visits for different problems and did not include return visits for the same illness. During the four years, 27 per cent of the Experimental College Program students and 18 per cent of the others (including 19 per cent of the volunteers who were not included in the ECP) had been hospitalized at least once ($X^2 = 4.34$, df 1, $p < .05$). Finally, the use of the psychiatric clinic also was consistently different. Thirty-four per cent of the Experimental College Program students and 22 per cent of the others visited a psychotherapist one or more times ($X^2 = 6.96$, df 1, $p < .01$). Table 3 makes it clear that the Experimental College Program experience differentiated the students who were accepted into the program from those who were in the regular program.

These differences can be understood on the basis of the personalization of the Experimental College student's experience. Since

Table 3

STUDENTS USING PSYCHIATRIC CLINIC, IN PER CENT

	Male	Female
Experimental College Program	34	35
Volunteers not included in ECP	15	21
Students not interested in ECP	26	23

students came to know our participant observer, a member of the staff of the Student Health Service, their relationship with him made the Student Health Service personally known to them, and they easily came to use its services. They did not know the participant observer as an official. In a personal relationship official identities recede as a sense of the person emerges.

Behavior is always an integration of a variety of factors and this behavior—the use of the Health Service—was no exception. The fact of psychiatric hospitalizations is interesting. There was a larger number of students in the ECP than in the regular program who were hospitalized for psychiatric reasons, and this difference in part contributes to the overall difference in frequency of hospitalization. Did the Experimental College experience make it more possible for students to encounter psychological difficulties? I do not think it did. The ECP was not appropriate for the level of development and integration of some students, and difficulties could and did arise from the influence of highly personal contacts. But these were individual matters, not related to the general characteristics of the program.

The Experimental College Program was not composed of a group particularly prone to psychiatric problems. Nor did anything suggest that these students were unusually prone to physical illnesses leading to more hospitalization and greater use of the medical clinics. They were, however, characterized by a readiness to explore, to interact with, and to make full use of their environment— a fact that may have contributed to their greater utilization of medical services. But their counterparts in the regular program exhibited similar qualities, and they did not make the same use of the facilities. Because students we interviewed from both the ECP and the regular program had met with us in our offices located in the Student Health Service hospital, they were similarly exposed to the existence and the possibilities of this part of the campus.

There was, however, a major difference: the Experimental College students *were acquainted with a representative of the Student Health Service.* Someone new to a city prefers to go to a physician, an attorney, or a psychotherapist recommended by a friend or acquaintance rather than to some unknown professional found through an impersonal referral agency. Similarly, the Experimental College students, enjoying a personal association with a member of the Student Health Service, felt easier about it and more readily came to use it. These observations of the students use of the campus health services suggest that the personalization of the experience in the ECP also might affect the students' feelings of relationship with other of the university's resources, leading them to a freer and fuller use of their possibilities than seemed to be the case with students in the regular program. Their academic performance in the junior and senior years supports this interpretation.

There was concern that the students spending their first two years in the Experimental College Program would be unprepared to cope with the pressures and timing of the regular courses when they went on to the third year. The data in Table 4 suggest that, on the contrary, as a group they were better prepared for course work in the junior and senior years than were students who had spent their first two years in the regular lower division.

Again, it is important to consider that many factors account for these differences. One may be that the students were stimulated by the need to change at the end of the second year. Students in the regular program progressed into the third year without a need to alter the pace and established style of their work. Students in the Experimental College Program, on the other hand, were faced with a new challenge at the beginning of the third year. They had to be alert to a new way of functioning, to learn its intricacies and conventions, and to adapt their style of work accordingly. Such a challenge could contribute to the student's level of functioning. But, however stimulating such a challenge might be, it probably would not sustain a higher level of performance throughout the last two

Table 4

ACADEMIC PERFORMANCE IN SECOND TWO YEARS

	Per Cent Earning B.A. Degree by December 1969 (End of Fourth Year)	Overall Grade Point Average at End of Fourth Year
Experimental College Program students	58	3.08
ECP students who transferred to regular program before completion of ECP	47	2.91
Volunteers not accepted in ECP	49	2.95
Students not interested in ECP	47	2.99

years. To account for the longevity of effect, some factor more fundamental to the educational process is implied.

Our data on the greater use of the health services and our knowledge of the experience in the ECP strongly suggest that it is the personalization of the educational experience—made possible by the Experimental College Program—that best accounts for the differences in functioning in the last two years. Professor Samuel Schaaf, one of the members of the faculty of the ECP, who compiled the data in Table 4, feels that the curriculum of the ECP was an equally influential part of the experiment. He once stated to me: "There was much soul searching regarding the meaning of education in relation to the curriculum problems." In other words, the students had a conscious opportunity to develop their attitudes toward education.

Personalization of experience apparently was important in the college life of the ECP students in yet another way. It contributed to an inclination to remain in school, although many students had attitudes typical of those who frequently withdraw in good standing.

During the two years of the ECP and during the entire four-year period as well, students who participated in the ECP withdrew from school less than did the other two groups in our sample. The rates of withdrawal during the entire period were 22.7 per cent for the ECP students, 34.1 per cent for their counterparts, and 34 per cent for the students in the regular program who did not volunteer for the ECP ($X^2 = 6.63$, df 2, $p < .05$). These withdrawal rates again seem clearly related to participation in the program.

As observed in previous work (Suczek and Alfert, 1965), and again in studying this group, students in the regular program who score in the highest quartile of the Social Maturity and the Impulse Expression scales have a higher rate of withdrawal than do students in the middle or low ranges of scores. Students in the ECP who scored in the highest quartile are an exception to this finding. Only 17 per cent withdrew, whereas 50 per cent of their counterparts withdrew, and 65 per cent of the students who did not volunteer for the ECP withdrew ($X^2 = 6.42$, df 2, $p < .05$).

What accounts for this striking relationship to participation in the ECP? The conventional grading system was abandoned in the ECP. Was it because failure was not possible? No. Students leaving the ECP did so of their own volition, but the proportion of those who left who were considered to be doing failing work was almost identical to the proportion of those who were failing who left the regular program. Differences in withdrawal rate were constant during the four years, and in the last two years all students were graded on their performances.

The fact of personalization was definitely important in reducing the withdrawal rate at least during the period of the ECP and probably during the entire four-years as well. The more personal experiences afforded by the ECP provided intrinsic values that could and did make academic tasks of more interest and impact.

The absence of grades in the ECP served, for some, to define the educational experience and the student's relationship to it in ways that probably affected their functioning throughout the remaining two years of college. In the ECP the students were relatively free from pressure, so many pursued varied personal and academic interests. Some registered for or audited other courses in the regular program; some became involved in close personal friendships; some explored and developed artistic or technical skills, or pursued hobbies such as photography. In a sense they seemed able to satisfy an extraordinary appetite for variety to a greater extent than was possible in the regular lower division program. Furthermore, they were better prepared to define and to become engaged in their subsequent academic pursuits.

Some students were captivated by the content of the academic program of the Experimental College. It was intrinsically interesting, and it had a clear relevance to contemporary life. Some students continued active thinking about the issues it raised and the questions it posed throughout their college years. Students had their most profound personal experiences with their teachers in the context of these issues.

Some of these issues were initiated by and insisted upon by Tussman—sometimes in the face of active opposition from other faculty members. His staunch defense of his position had, itself, considerable impact on the students. They saw him as insistent in the presentation of the issues—sometimes with great patience, sometimes with none. They saw him in despair when he felt his efforts were being subverted or diverted by competing student or faculty interests. They saw him pleased when students were responsive to his efforts, whether agreeing or disagreeing. As is made clear by one student in the following discussion, this visibility of Tussman's character in all its aspects helped bring to life for the students a sense of the essential humanity of affairs of the past.

In this excerpt taken from one of the group discussions at the end of the senior year, three of the four students present participated as speakers. The first speaker (1) is a young man who was not admitted into the ECP. Immediately prior to the group discussion he had been trying to learn about it from the others, members of the ECP. The second student speaker is a man (2) and the third (3) is a woman.

1: *Would you have found, though, the program to be significantly different or maybe more valuable if instead of it being the Tussman program it was, say, the Professor A program or the Professor B program?*

2: Oh well, then it wouldn't have been it. I think it takes that kind of a personality to organize something like that.

1: No. Assuming that, in other words, all I'm saying is—let's say that Tussman was the grand administrator. All right, let's say the program could take place without Tussman as an individual somewhere.

2: You mean that he would be the chancellor of the program.

1: Yes, chancellor of the program—aside from the head academic individual. All I'm saying is, what would the Tussman program have been like without Tussman?

2: Somebody ought to run a program like that and find out.

1: Do you think it would be a particularly valuable experience? Do you think it would be more valuable?

2: Anything is a valuable experience in that sort of intensity.

3: I learned a lot from Tussman. I mean, I disliked his authoritarian bit, but he's sort of a sporadic genius. You really get so that you can feel for the guy because there are moments when he's really down, and then there are moments when he's just brilliant. And it really is a neat thing to learn about a man like Tussman.

2: Yeah, he was a great guy to be around. I got burned up at him because he'd come out with very irresponsible statements.

1: A very responsible person.

2: Yes, that may be. I don't know. Certainly was a most—the first year the two important characters were Professor A and Tussman. I've had a lot to do with Professor A since then. I haven't had much to do with Tussman. But in some respects, in that instance, Tussman came off as a more, if not powerful, more memorable character. He wasn't stronger than Professor A, especially in their arguments—also in the contact that you had with him—but he somehow was more—I thought he was a rounder character than—the personality that showed had more facets.

1: I have known Professor A well. Professor A as an individual, though, is one of these, incredibly sometimes, quiet individuals You get the idea he's kind of leading you places without ever saying anything, and doesn't really assert himself as an individual.

2: Sometimes gets kind of stale.

3: Well, I thought it was interesting because Tussman considered the program and education to be character development. I mean that was his big thing—character development.

2: It was the biggest because it was a mistake.

3: No. To me, Tussman is a character and he taught us that, I think, about people. Like when we were studying seventeenth century England, one of the major things we had to do was look at, like, Milton or Hobbes, I forget who all the characters were, and through the personality of that person to understand the age—in other words, what was going on in the time.

1: That now—I won't even say now—that has been for a long time the standard procedure in English departments. Because that's true. You can't understand Plato unless you basically understand his basic set of assumptions and look at what he's saying.

2: Which is really sort of a philosophical—

1: The point is, I've had long arguments with professors on that same level, as whether or not that's even worth doing.

3: Yes, but without BSing about it, because of the character of Tussman, you could grasp something about this other, the whole bit about what was going on.

Tussman's intensity of feeling regarding the program and the students is expressed by another student in another discussion group. The student obviously is ambivalent but nevertheless respects Tussman's dedication to a principle.

Tussman had this guiding idea behind the Tussman program. This was his—you know—I don't know what—like your magnum opus or something. And in some respects, I think it's good what he made us do, the way he made us read certain things and conform to his ideas. I don't think it worked out as successfully probably as he, you know, had envisaged. You remember—I don't remember whether he told us this in lecture or what—but he was talking about when Meiklejohn had his experiment at Wisconsin, and Meiklejohn said that he wanted, if the kids in his college—as I recall they lived together—if they were awakened in the middle of the night and there was a fire, he said he wanted the first thing

*for them to say when the person said, "Who are you?"—you know,
when they woke him up—he wanted the student to reply, "I'm a
member of the Experimental College." And I had the impression
that Tussman said that, you know, that was what he had in mind
and obviously it didn't work. We were all just too, too much individuals. It never could have worked with that group because the
whole reason we were in there was because we didn't want to be in,
you know, this rigid group business. But, in some senses, I think,
you know, Tussman was right. If he had turned me loose and said,
"All right, say whatever you want to," I just wasn't ready for that
yet.*

Different teachers engaged student curiosity in different
ways. Tussman—repetitive and even dogmatic about his principles
and views concerning authority and responsibility—impressed students with the strength of his convictions. Students grew tired, at
times, of the issues themselves but were attracted to the emotion
behind the issues. Another teacher aroused their interest because he
possessed a very different quality. He never appeared to take an
absolute position, but instead he always seemed to be opening up
new possibilities, drawing the student on to consider new ideas,
pointing out to him new perspective. He was constantly in motion
and never came to intellectual rest. Students generally responded
positively to him, being both stimulated mentally and entertained
by the complex interrelationships of his thoughts (which usually
were presented in an anecdotal, discursive manner). Some students,
hoping to discover absolutes, were made anxious by the broad span
of his thinking and its apparent lack of final answers.

In their senior year, the students were asked to indicate, for
each academic year, which professor, if any, was outstanding. Of
the eight teachers in the ECP, three account for 83 per cent of the
choices made by the students during the time they were in the program. The choices are, roughly, evenly divided among the three.
From our observations and student reports, we also know that these
three accounted for most of the tension and interaction among the
faculty. One, needless to say, was Tussman. The second was with
the program only for the first year and was more interested in dis-
covering and learning as a process than in establishing an absolute

truth. At the beginning of the program, when each faculty member was to speak to the entire college assembly about his favorite passage in the *Iliad*, he stated, "No matter where you cut it, if the work is alive you draw blood. I don't have a favorite passage; it may be different every day." It was his proposal to read Hobbes for its literary merit rather than for its elucidation or revelation of the truth (of the social contract) that led to the most severe crisis of the first year (see Chapter Four). The students were acutely aware of this conflict. Many were strongly attracted to this man. Stimulated by his influence, they produced good work both in the ECP and in the regular program, where they later sought out and enrolled in his courses.

A third faculty member also conflicted with some of Tussman's basic points of view, but in a different way. He tended to encourage the students to question everything, to emphasize the relativity of things, and to analyze them logically. His dialectical influence prevailed primarily during the second year of the program.

The dynamic interaction of these three men was meaningful to the students. The students' responses were not always favorable, but even when negative or fearful, they were strong.

In the following group, two of the five students were discussing their experiences in the Program. The first speaker, a young woman, is referring to Tussman:

1: *But I just don't think he's a very nice person. And I guess that, you know, that colored my whole opinion of the program. And I know that I'm not the only one who feels that way.*
2: *Right.*
Group leader: What's nice? What's a nice person?
1: *Professor A. Or Professor B.*
2: *Well, I've, well, finally about the whole program—I mean, I don't even absolve those two men. I think that what the program was about was—it's sort of like, these naive little kids came to Berkeley, and they put up—I mean, it was like the Olympic pantheon. It was just, you know, these great gods were sitting there giving the word, and we were supposed to believe it all and take it all in and deal with it on their level. And they were just—*

*1: No, I don't think Professor B said that at all. Professor B's main
point was to question everything you were told, never to accept
anything blindly, but—*

2: Except him.

1: No, I—

2: Well.

Group Leader: Go ahead.

1: But you're right in Tussman's case.

*2: Well, I think it was true of all of them. I mean, they all came
on in a different way. I mean, Professor A was a storyteller. He
told wonderful stories. And by the time he got through, your
mind was blank and you said, "Say, that's really great! Where'd
you think of that?" But you had nothing to say. I mean, you felt
like there was nothing you could possibly add, because here was
this experienced, wise man who could tell stories and they were
interesting. And Professor B, the thing that he did that I found
absolutely impossible, was he was so rational that he would pursue something to its logical absurdity, and he would turn life into
this, you know. It was like an equation. And life isn't like that.
He couldn't accept anything that was irrational. You would have
to pursue it in a logical way. And unless you said, "Yes, you're
right!" then the conversation just, you know, it went on—
dragged on for hours and it was just, didn't mean anything. And
the thing was, is that, I mean, well, more than any class I've ever
been in since, or before, it was like there was the person who
spoke and you sat and listened to them, because they knew, or
something like that. I don't know. I don't know why it was like
that. But I've never experienced that.*

The group discussions during the senior year made it evident
that the students were very attentive to their teachers. They were
alert to a teacher's willingness to state the truth as he saw it, to
express his standards and to insist upon them. They were aware of
a teacher's moral courage when he publicly disagreed with others.
Clearly, what the teacher tries to accomplish by means of his
curriculum—"to develop [our] rational powers, to heighten sensitivity to and awareness of fundamental human problems, to culti-
vate and strengthen the habits and dispositions which make possible

for humanity to displace the varieties of warfare with the institutions, the practices, and the spirit of reasoning together," in short to fit the student for "the life of active membership in the democratic community" (Tussman, 1969)—he may accomplish as well by the example of his own behavior.

The students in the ECP observed the day-by-day and week-by-week collaboration, conflicts, and efforts at resolution among the faculty and between them and the teaching assistants. Because of weekly meetings and biweekly seminars with one professor during an entire semester, the students had an unusual opportunity to observe a teacher in his setting. They saw him as a competent teacher, academician and scholar. They saw him in immediate juxtaposition with his colleagues, where contrasts could be sharply drawn. They saw him as a person—a man with foibles, weaknesses, and blind spots and also with special virtues. They were aware of the personal lives of the faculty: who was married and to whom, who had children, who played what sports, who was having personal difficulties. This information was available through direct observation and via the grapevine.

An immediate effect of the exposure to different styles and disagreements among the faculty was to make relative the contents of study—the ideas under consideration. The direct experience of different points of view, strongly held and defended, undoubtedly underscored the complexity of the concepts that were studied. Furthermore, intimate view of a teacher provided opportunity to examine personal qualities that were admired and internalized. Such exposure may have resulted in much more than was readily discernable at the time. People may not be aware of what use they have made of such experience until later in their lives. But, at least, it will reveal the teacher as a human being who, as one student put it, "doesn't eat Ph.D., doesn't have a Ph.D. refrigerator, and whose garden doesn't have all the names engraved in Latin."

This statement, of course, idealizes the possibilities inherent in a highly personalized experience such as that existing in the experimental program. I can point to some students for whom it was clearly a good experience: one in which the teacher discerned the developmental tasks with which the student was coping and, accordingly, was able to help him with them. But the contrary also is true. I will cite two examples of experiences, unfortunate or bad in the sense that they probably impeded the students' development.

One young woman was in the process—as young people her age often are—of establishing herself as an independent person. She was from a middle-class family living in a large metropolitan area. Her father was a professional man. Here is how she described her family: "Father is a liberal but has fixed ideas—sort of a strong person around the household. Mother is not well educated—one year of college. She plays bridge, gets her hair done. She doesn't have much to stand on. Always agrees with father; has middle-class attitudes. If there is anything important I want to discuss with them I have to wait till father comes home. I'm more close to father, maybe."

Her description of family relationships suggested a prevailing stiffness and stickiness with little pleasure or comfort at home. Everyone took himself seriously, it would appear, and the parents were possessive. The girl had had a lot of trouble with her parents. They appeared to argue at length over relatively trifling matters— the appropriate length of time for telephone calls, for example. Their arguments decreased in time, but the girl's parents still made it clear that they disapproved of many of her views. During the same period they were upset by the behavior of her brother who had been getting bad grades in the tenth grade, who had joined peace groups, would not get his hair cut, went barefoot, and finally was suspended from school. Apparently he deliberately took a position that was far removed from his family's ideals.

The girl liked "pretty much everything" during her first year in the program. It was the first time she had been a long way from home, and she was "pretty happy, although I hated the dorms." She was not especially attractive—she obviously carried the burden of too many pounds. In her first interview we perceived her as lonely and depressed. She appeared, however, not to be thinking much about her own unhappy state but to be diverting her concern to the unhappy state she perceived in the society in which she lived. Some of her feelings about her family probably were reflected in the intensity of her statement: "I have always hated the American system and all its injustices."

She had difficulty making friends. In high school she had had "my own close little group," but actually engaged in few activities beyond classes and reading. She did, however, undertake some political activities. After a year and a half of college—in spite of meeting different people in the program—she still had not made friends. She described herself as quiet and shy around new people.

Obviously, she was a young person basically attached to and involved with her family. She longed to please them but seemed unable to do so. "I cannot be a solid, stable, unchanging, faithful individual—as my parents seem to wish me to be." She was experiencing difficulty separating herself from her parents. The process was thwarted because of their possessiveness and her own fear of entering into new relationships. She found little satisfaction in relations with her family and peers. She was shy, lonesome, and longing for a purpose or direction in life. She took on the problems of society—especially American society—as her special burden. She devoted time and energy to political campaigning and probably gained a sense of identity and belonging in the process. But by the time she came to Berkeley she was discouraged by politics and did not participate in a very popular "peoples' candidate" campaign toward the end of her first year.

In the experimental program she was one of the less visible students. Her papers in the first year were conventional in content and style and somewhat naive. She was regarded, however, as very intelligent and serious. In her second year she became interested in a teacher, one who also was specially interested in political activity. Papers she wrote for him bore attached notes containing observations about how she felt about the assignment, about writing the paper, and so forth. An early note had a postscript: "I think I would like to talk to you on a personal level sometime." One of her last papers incorporated personal messages so that, in effect, it was a personal communication between herself and the teacher. No doubt she regarded his as a sympathetic ear. The teacher talked with her at some length, especially about political philosophies. His ensuing comments did not indicate that he was unusually interested in her. In his evaluation he said, "I am sure she will develop in time—she should become a first-rate student." Apparently he responded to her political interests rather than to her individuality. Nevertheless, she said she felt "turned on" by his attentions and interest.

She said, "In two quarters, without even trying—in fact, probably without even knowing it—he regenerated (*sic*) more political consciousness in me than I'd ever had."

She began reading avidly outside the curriculum, reviving an interest in socialist philosophy which her teacher shared. She joined the massive student strike against Navy recruiters in December 1966 and was active in the Spring Mobilization against the Vietnam War (April 1967). She met people from groups adhering to various socialist doctrines. One young man became interested in her and gave her readings and took her to lectures sponsored by his group.

Once the girl's teacher responded to her loneliness by suggesting that she combine her interests by joining a political organization to find a group of like-minded friends who would help her feel less alone. The idea touched the essence of her troubles. The group offered a way of self-determination by clearly differentiating herself from her family and simultaneously gaining companionship. She joined.

Her parents were very disappointed and insisted that she return home for the summer. She did. In the fall—the start of her third year—she became involved with the young man who had introduced her to the activities of his group. He, several years her senior, took part in protest activity; he neither worked for a living nor attended school; he lived a nomadic life. She was impressed by his interest in her and found it difficult not to respond. His style of life was completely different from any she had known—she was attracted by his attention but feared his way of life. Her family forbade her to see him. During her third year, therefore, she kept him and her political activities a secret from her parents. They literally bribed her with the gift of a car to maintain their own values.

At the end of her final year, the girl was depressed and unhappy. She stated that "things are not going well." She left her companion, in part because of physical abuse but mainly because he represented a more radical change in life style than she could tolerate. She withdrew from political activity and the political group she had joined. Apparently her fellow members were too extreme and provided only temporary surcease from her sense of social isolation. She was disillusioned and interested in nothing, the idea of graduating was distressing, and she had no idea what she was going to do. She wanted to go to a psychotherapist for help but stated that, because of her father's disapproval, she could not bring herself to do so.

During four years she seemed to have made no progress in asserting her independence. She began the program with a particularly difficult developmental problem. Although the personal relationship she sought out with her teacher may have offered possible help, his response, unfortunately, was in terms of his own political interests. It did not take into account the personal significance their relationship had for her nor the nature and extent of her developmental needs. His encouragement, therefore, urged her to take a position so extreme that it became intolerable both to her family and herself. It made her already difficult task more difficult and she retreated from it.

Another student, a young man of considerable talent, had a different experience but also one that contributed little to, and possibly complicated, the satisfactory accomplishment of his development. His experience centered around the fact that, because of his facility in thought and expression, he made quick and favorable impressions on most people. As a result he did not find it necessary to expend much effort to gain the regard many other students worked very hard to achieve. The teacher in the program with whom he came in close personal contact inspired him to do some of his best work. This teacher had a special respect for the autonomy of the individual. He always stated his own views openly and unequivocally but never demanded that they be accepted as absolute truths or generally valid. He was convinced that his students' opinions could be defended as equally valid. He wanted to discover the nature of those opinions and encouraged students to understand and develop them. He was clear in criticizing the quality of a student's work, both its excellence and shortcomings. He suggested improvements but eschewed requiring a student to perform as prescribed. Here is his first impression of the student under discus-

sion: "Possesses some of the most important qualities of a writer
. . . he will need practice writing. Promise: brilliant. Prescription:
write, write, WRITE."

The evaluation prepared by this teacher and his teaching
assistant at the end of the first semester (and given to the student)
reflected the same qualities in the student: "We know that when
. . . begins to hit on all cylinders, he will be a tremendously dynamic thinker, writer, and possibly actor. At present, however, there
is a certain tentativeness which manifests itself in having his papers
halt just short of where, by the logic of things, they should go." At
the end of the second year of the program the evaluation was
written by a different teacher: "An obviously bright and energetic
boy who writes well and has ideas. Paper somewhat disappointing,
probably because he didn't spend much time on it. The most interesting student I had this quarter." Clearly no one had made any
real demands on this student, challenges to force him to experience
his own power and his capacity to decide where and how to use it.

In his intellectual biography at the end of the program he
mused about the problems of producing good writing. He observed
that he had not written well since his first paper for the teacher by
whom he was clearly inspired. He asked himself whether he should
continue to write good papers, or, "is it natural to perform best
under optimum conditions which occur sporadically?" He concluded that, without optimal conditions, he could not "tune in" to
a subject and produce a really good paper. In other words, he felt
he could not write well at his own volition.

After the program concluded, he progressed to the upper
division, showing great ingenuity and imagination in the development of his own curriculum. He was able to use the regular program as an opportunity for thorough involvement in areas of study
that particularly interested him without jeopardizing his academic
standing. In essence, he was able to concentrate on one course without doing poorly in others. (In this regard he demonstrated very
well that education in a large institution need not consist merely
of routine prerequisites, requirements, and majors. With a little
extra work, the educational program has the flexibility to be put to
imaginative use in the pursuit of personal objectives.)

At the end of his senior year, however, this student still was pursuing the answer to the same question with which he came to the university. Put simply, it was, "Do I *have* to?" That year he enrolled for independent study with the professor he met in the experimental program and with whom he continued to have a close personal relationship. As is customary in independent study, the student came in to discuss what he was doing, thinking, and working on. But he did not turn in work. He began to assume, apparently, that it was unnecessary to turn in work to earn a "pass" or a passing grade. He was astonished and dismayed when he did not graduate because, in this course his work was graded "incomplete." It is significant that he chose his favorite teacher for an eleventh hour effort to find himself. At 12:01 his trusted friend said, "You *do* have to, and you *can!*"

In such experiences, apparently close personal associations enable the faculty to perceive a student's problems and dilemmas and respond appropriately to them, but even under the best circumstances, there is no guarantee that the appropriate response will always occur.

A conclusion, nevertheless, is unavoidable: the personalization of the experience in the ECP generated a different view of and response to the university, and many of its segments seemed more vital and meaningful by virtue of personal relationships. The extensive use of the Student Health Service, resulting from the students' personal—although casual—acquaintance with a member of its staff—is an example of the action a personal relationship can generate. Thus, as a result of personalization, the overall dropout rate was relatively low among the students in the ECP. Furthermore, those vital, talented, and independent students who have been observed to be those most likely to drop out apparently felt meaningfully engaged by the program and, consequently, remained at the university. (Under other circumstances they were almost self-compelled to leave the academy.) Not only did such students remain in larger numbers, but more of them completed their work for a degree earlier and functioned at a higher level than did students who spent their first two years in the relatively impersonal lower division.

The personal friendships that developed between students and members of the faculty often continued throughout the student's

stay at the university. They provided personal continuity for the
student (and the teacher as well), and sometimes afforded an opportunity to confront problems central to a student's full development.

Finally, we could see that some of the students we interviewed from both programs developed more meaningful relationships to their education through their contacts with us, the researchers. Although we were not identified by the students as being
part of the university and our contacts with them were brief and
relatively formal, some students made it clear that we helped provide an otherwise unencountered focus in their college life.

Essentially, the curriculum and structure of the Experimental
College Program intended to develop an understanding of the relationship between freedom and responsibility: to point out that in
the process of maintaining the rules of society one provides oneself
the freedom to live within that society. I have no evidence to indicate how well this particular lesson was learned. However, evidence
that I have presented in this chapter suggests that a related and
perhaps more fundamental lesson was learned. I am suggesting it is
through personal relationships that one becomes fully free to experience oneself and the world and realize that the responsibility for
maintaining a personal relationship is essential both to social and
individual survival.

The specific question with which I began this chapter—how
does a student develop a full appreciation of himself as an individual
in relationship with others?—remains unanswered in any specific
detail. I have, however, one further observation relative to this:
regardless of their particular educational experience at Berkeley,
most students in this study had a strong sense of community commitment when they entered college. These students, whatever
actions or plans they contemplated for themselves, were concerned
with the question, "What will this do for my community?" It is my
opinion that their high value of personal involvement with the
community sprang, at least in part, from the middle-class society
in which they grew up: There children and adolescents are not
needed to fill useful functions. These young men and women, therefore, may be intent—more so than were previous generations—on
establishing for themselves an important role in the community.

In light of the importance of personalization in the Experimental College Program, two major developments currently being fostered in higher education should be considered: one is a tendency to more depersonalization of the educational experience and the other is a tendency to more personalization.

The first best may be described as an industrialization of the educational process emphasizing the development of various programs and innovations intended to accelerate communication of information and techniques. Programs of "continuing education" which utilize the single, abbreviated course (in academic argot, the "mini-course") or the symposium (often involving only a day or two of time) belong in this category. The new "external degree" programs, too often conceived as little more than conventional courses or groups of courses televised and piped into homes, also are of this sort: a change of locus that does increase the distance—and not merely physically—between teacher and student, since it loses absolutely the important, creative effect of interpersonal interaction.

In a similar vein, within existing curricula there is a tendency to accelerate by means of the challenge examination or by a course repackaged into smaller units (which the student presumably can master by himself). The overall intention of this design is to liberate the student from the temporal lock-step of regular semester systems. A report fostering these kinds of development is Carnegie Commission on Higher Education (1971). Similar educational programs, many of which also make use of programmed instruction, tend to limit or exclude personal experiences with the teacher.

An opposite, second development is increasing personalization of the educational experience. The cluster colleges attempt to facilitate close relationships between students, and especially between students and faculty over an extended period of time. The cluster colleges as well as some briefer undergraduate programs which emphasize a community of learning (for example, the college within a college) are the models for this stream of development. Various examples are described in Gaff (1970). In these efforts, the intentions often are dual: first, to provide personal relationships in which learning can take place and, second, to make possible—in teacher-student relationships—a greater individualization of the educational process.

It seems reasonable to conclude that the first kind of development in higher education will contribute to growing technological development in our society. To the degree that we emphasize the second kind of development, we may be more assured that our society will survive to enjoy the fruits of its technology.

Chapter 10

Patterns of Development During College

*A*s important as personalization is in its effect on a student's educational experience, it does not account for development and change in his personality. There is, on the contrary, a dazzling array of variables to confound the researcher. The student lives within a varied context: his academic work, his peers and his teachers, institutions on campus and in the surrounding community, society at large. His contextual dimensions are not exclusively spatial; there is an important factor of temporality; there is a sense of living with past experiences, including,

131

above all, those with his family. Occasionally, when we came to know a student well during his years in college, we were able to glimpse some interplay of these factors as they affected the course of the student's development. Often we discerned important themes in the student's experience—that is, what evoked his responses— but we never knew how these were related to the past. At times we despaired, feeling we had gained no understanding of the person.

Through observation we distinguished predominantly two changes in the students under study: one occurred spontaneously and un-self-consciously; the other was a change that students deliberately seemed to seek. These two patterns, to be reviewed in detail, emerged clearly only later in the study. Initially, our impressions of change were scattered, sometimes bewilderingly so. At times students seemed not to be changing at all, and other times students were undergoing such rapid changes that it was difficult to follow them and understand in the least what it was they were experiencing. Strong impressions gained in the first two interviews might be revised, perhaps radically, during a third meeting with a student.

We did not attempt to organize an explicitly stated theory from our observations. Had I done so, it probably would have been as follows: Change springs from action. Acting, experiencing, and dealing with objects—physical and symbolic—brings new knowledge of oneself and one's world; new meanings, cause-and-effect understandings, and ways of behaving emerge. An expanding repertory of experiences—of possibilities for behavior and action— most predictably results when someone with a predisposition to change encounters a new situation that challenges him to discover new ways of behaving. If the challenge, however, is too great, the result may intensify familiar forms of behavior.

We observed the workings of these principles in the changes that took place in ourselves as well as in our subjects, the students. We initially pursued our study according to our original assumptions and methods. As time went on, I, at least, did not allow myself to contemplate mounting indications of inconsistency and contradiction in our methods and observations. My tendency was to ignore them and thrust them out of my thoughts. Eventually, however, their dissonance compelled me to admit that I had changed my views on many important aspects of the study. As a result we were led—perhaps *forced* in the interest of intellectual honesty—to revise our original questions and methods.

The revision involved recognizing that the original concept of the study implicitly conceived the student as involved in affairs essentially circumscribed by the campus and his home community. To use so limited a concept, however, was to tear the student from the context of his real world—a world whose boundaries far exceeded those of our original speculations. As the study proceeded it was plain that the pace of change that was shaping society at large also was profoundly influencing our subjects. It was affecting more than our subjects—it was affecting us, the researchers, and also our study. Nothing appeared standing still: everything was in motion.

In an earlier section (Chapter Seven) I demonstrated that the students who entered the university in 1965 responded to our questionnaire very differently from those who entered in 1961. There was other evidence, gathered from observations and from interviews to support the original observation of this difference. To understand some aspects of the changing attitudes we found in our students, we felt we must consider in detail the particular cultural events and changes through which the students were living and in the context of which they were defining their world.

During the four-year period there were two assassinations of prominent American leaders—Martin Luther King and Robert Kennedy; the Vietnam War was escalated from a "technical advisor" level to one involving 500,000 combat troops with 40,000 casualties; Watts and other ghetto communities exploded. In addition, the Berkeley campus was wracked by a dozen major crises that sometimes paralyzed the regular activities of the campus community for days at a time and often involved violence—by both young people and the authorities. Such events inevitably affect social institutions, the frequency of their occurrence adding a compelling quality that is impossible to ignore.

Dramatic events—heralding and indicating social change —occurred in the fifties, it is true. The Korean War, the conflicts of the Joseph McCarthy era, and the loyalty oath controversy on the Berkeley campus were prominent examples. Yet students of the fifties seemed, by and large, uninterested and unaffected by those events. Apparently exposure alone was not enough. The young people entering college during the sixties, on the other hand, seemed to feel an increasing urge to participate. Involvement became a creed—a motivating force directing their mode of living.

We can speculate about reasons for the greater involvement of our students in the events of their world as compared with the previous generation of students: they were born after the Bomb, when a problematic future urged humans to emphasize more strongly than heretofore the immediate present; there emerged an atmosphere of immediacy, of action, and a corresponding rejection of the old pattern of postponing present gratification in the interests of future accomplishment and satisfaction. These students grew up, for the most part, in a society and era of material exuberance—one in which few individuals in the classes that customarily were privileged to go to college experienced much in the way of physical deprivation—in a sense they never needed to focus on survival but had the luxury of latitude to concentrate on other involvements. (And, as I suggested in the previous chapter, they did not serve any useful function.) They were raised, as a group, under the aegis of child-rearing practices symbolized by Dr. Spock. They were free; they were encouraged to express themselves. There were, to be sure, misunderstandings and overreactions to Dr. Spock's position. Freedom of self-expression occasionally was pushed to extremes: if children wished to draw on the wall with crayons, walls were made washable. It was better (and often possible) to change the environment rather than to inhibit the child. Rather than to be "seen and not heard," we encouraged—even urged—children to express their thoughts and feelings on an equal status with adults. The government of the family often was commonly decided on a democratic one-man one-vote basis regardless of the age of its participants. Both action and engagement were encouraged. Such encouragement could lead to various consequences—an increase in a motivation for active involvement seems certain.

Even though these students grew up in the gloomy atmosphere of the Cold War era, their society, meanwhile, expressed, in a number of ways, an optimistic and idealistic regard for individual human rights and values. While they were still in grammar school, the Supreme Court handed down its epochal decision on desegregation. By the time they were entering high school, black students were attempting to implement that decision by boycotting movie houses and staging sit-ins at uncooperative restaurants. The Peace Corps was established, offering what seemed a fresh new way to be of service to underprivileged people. Medicare was being organized and put into effect as they were starting college.

Many, of course, were relatively untouched by political and social concerns; they matured in an atmosphere of carefree and playful adolescence. In California there was a cult with a passion to surf: they learned to ride in front of the turbulence of the waves —poised precariously and defiantly—as they surged toward land. The surfers could stand on top of the moving force and conquer it by means of their own fragile but commanding physical prowess. They could feel themselves, perhaps, as masters of fate—riding ahead of, and possibly in control of, the forces of change. Regardless of their tastes and interests, by the time all these students were in high school they were listening to Bob Dylan and his dramatic songs of social protest: the answers to social injustice, he informed them, were already "blowin' in the wind." It is probably significant that in 1965, Dylan's were the most popular records sold in shops near the campus. Finally, as a point of anguished exclamation, on the eve of the juvenile period of the students' lives, Medgar Evers and John Kennedy were assassinated.

Major attitudinal and value changes were taking place in society, and this generation of students was attending to those changes in new ways. These students were more attentive than were previous generations to such changes and were more inclined to respond to them directly, actively, and immediately. Compared with their predecessors studied earlier (Sanford, 1962; Katz, 1968), this group indicated definite tendencies to greater awareness and greater involvement in world events, community events, and changing values. In prior generations of students, individuals looked to the campus community to discover models for the selves they wished to become. This new generation seemed also to eye the whole world, with special attention to the international world of late adolescence and young adulthood.

We were able to observe several major changes in values that seemed attributable to the changing pattern of involvement. For example, our students tended to hold in very high value the idea of contributing to the welfare of their community and they frequently engaged themselves in activities with that objective in mind. They also indicated a readiness to adopt new values, to change themselves and their modes of living. There appeared to be an eager receptivity—at times almost a *quest*—for new ways and new ideas. Such an attitude seemed to lead quite naturally to a positive valuing —even an idealization—of change; one side effect, apparently, being that complaints about the status quo (whatever it might be) and the establishment were almost programmatic.

Our observations suggest that these young men and women were relatively more involved with their community than were students previously. Sanford, describing data from the study by Katz, concludes, "in 1965 most of the seniors were apathetic about political issues" (1967, pp. 69–70). He adds, "When these same students were asked to list the organizations and clubs that had been most important to them during their college years, very small proportions (never more than 10 per cent) listed groups for civil rights or for other political study or action."

The students in our study, on campus during the four years following those of which Sanford wrote, indicated a very different state of affairs. When asked to list all activities other than academic ones, 65 per cent of the men and 83 per cent of the women included participation in one or more community or political activities. These were conventional political activities on campus and in the community, as well as participation in organizing protests such as the Spring Mobilization, demonstrations, and strikes on campus. Community activities included volunteer work in ghetto schools and playgrounds, in half-way houses, in draft counseling centers, and the like. Paid community work was not counted in our summary of these activities. (In light of such involvement, it was interesting that in our group discussions many students expressed feelings of helplessness about being able to change anything in the world.)

From our group discussions at the end of the senior year (May 1969), we realized that an idea of contributing to the welfare of the community was emerging as a strongly valued ethic. During the period we interviewed the Berkeley students for the Katz study (1961–1965), we were impressed by students' prevailing interest in their own, personal, future well-being and private achievements and satisfactions. Altruism was apparently at a minimum. Such emphasis on privatism—and the apparent lack of interest in public affairs—on the part of students in the fifties and early sixties has been well described in previous studies (Feldman and Newcomb, 1969).

The students in our study, when thinking about their plans for the future, frequently considered the question, "How will this activity—this work—this career—contribute to the betterment of the community?" "Community" might refer to their city, their sub-culture, the nation as a whole, and sometimes the world. Whether implicit or explicit in their thinking, this question seemed to be a natural, taken-for-granted consideration in making one's plans. Significantly, it was a component of the thinking of individuals with widely divergent future plans: practice of law, academic scholarship, biological research, teaching, exploring revolutionary new ways of living. It is interesting to note, parenthetically, that student drug use was by this time, to a large extent, a communal or social experience: LSD typically was taken with another person present to serve as "guide" for the "trip," and a marijuana "joint" was shared among all those present.

In the course of our study we came to realize that 1) rapid cultural change was taking place during the most intense develop-mental period of our students' lives; 2) partly as a consequence of this change they developed a greater capacity for involvement in the events and changes in their world; 3) their awareness of changing values and their ready adoption of new values appeared to be ac-celerating, certainly as compared with the generation arriving at college four years earlier; and 4) contributing to community better-ment was an emergent social value.

Another example of changing values is found in our students' attitudes towards education. In the fifties it was still accepted that a college degree and an education were synonymous. In the early sixties this concept of a college education was being challenged by some of the more questioning students, and the challenge burgeoned into a major issue in higher education. Many students in college began to feel that they must choose between one of these objectives —acquire an education or earn a degree. But to these students they were not only separable but possible mutually exclusive goals. Our data suggest that the students, while still in high school, already became cognizant of the issue and formed opinions relative to it prior to their arrival in college.

In the late fifties the most common complaint made by college students about their courses was "too much work." By the middle sixties the complaint had changed: a new fashionable complaint was that the work was "irrelevant." It was as though the students developed a greater independence and self-assertiveness and were proclaiming, "I can do the work, but I'm not sure that I want to." It appeared that our 1965 freshmen arrived at Berkeley with these attitudes already well incorporated in their thinking.

Complaining characterized these students. They complained about many aspects of their society and their lives. Indeed, we found complaining to be so prevalent that we speculated that it might represent an unusually intense effort on the part of these young people to differentiate themselves from the older generation —the generation that had tried so hard not to differentiate children from adults. The rejection of everyone "over thirty" seemed, perhaps, a manifestation of such differentiating (and identifying) efforts.

Complaining about the academic experience almost was a cultural requirement, obligatory among students of this era. Their almost universal, stereotypical response when asked about their four years in college was that it was "largely a waste of time;" it was "irrelevant"; it "prevented" them from "thinking" and from "reading anything in depth"; and it "contributed nothing" to their personal or intellectual growth—matters which they attended to, they claimed, elsewhere.

However, in general discussions the same students remarked, almost as consistently, on experiences with teachers and courses which had, in their words, "turned them on." The senior year questionnaire asked them to indicate outstanding experiences of that nature. There were virtually no negative experiences reported. Eighty per cent reported good experiences with from one to five of their teachers and in one to five separate courses during the four years. In other words, the majority had enough good experiences to average out to about one per semester. This seemed to be an unusually fine record for any institution, but particularly for one the size of Berkeley.

Cultural change raised serious questions for our study. The Impulse Expression (IE) Scale, one of the scales on which we relied to measure personality changes, was developed ten years earlier (during the early 1950s). Psychologists developing methods for studying college students at that time considered *expression of impulse* a positive value in the psychological makeup of the average student, who was viewed as arriving at college as rather an inhibited, docile, conventional fellow, out of tune—for the most part—with his fantasy, imagination, and feelings. It was assumed that, in his development into a more complex and integrated person, he would become aware, during college, of these resources within himself and learn to make them part of his functioning. The IE scale hence was designed to measure this developmental change.

The idea of expression of impulses has become essentially reified, positively and more or less unquestioningly valued by most young and many older persons: it now is a social value that sometimes is pursued with a vengeance. Those who view themselves as inadequate in self-expression may seek therapeutic help to overcome the "deficiency." Clearly, in such a climate, responses by contemporary students to the items of the IE scale must be interpreted differently from those of students during the fifties.

Our male students—as freshmen—had mean scores on both the F (Authoritarianism) scale and the E (Ethnocentrism) scale significantly lower than those of seniors graduating the same year. We could not give this datum the same interpretation for freshmen that we could for seniors. We could not interpret this to mean that students coming to Berkeley in 1965 were necessarily complexly developed, flexible, and able to tolerate conflict and difference in themselves and others to the degree that their scores would indicate. We could not infer personality qualities for them such as we might for seniors. Many attitudes which reflect basic personality dispositions identified with the Authoritarianism and Ethnocentrism syndromes have been identified and overtly questioned in the process of changing social attitudes that occurred during the lifetime of our students. They are attitudes that many, especially young, persons now consciously eschew. The students' response to the E scale is based on attitudes about minorities and outgroups that are very different from those prevailing in the forties when these measures were first standardized.

In other words, test results that for one generation could be accepted as indicating a set of genuine and unself-conscious attitudes, were thrown into doubt for the next generation because between the two generations a basic change occurred in social propriety: it was no longer socially acceptable to hold many ideas and attitudes previously taken for granted.

In like fashion, the idea of change became an integral part of contemporary ideology, especially that of the college population. The liberal arts college always has had the stated purpose of facilitating development of young people into mature, wise, and well-functioning citizens of the world: to transform students by teaching them. And if a number of students in any graduating class are recognized as liberally educated persons—that is, free to function with intelligent adaptation to life's problems—then educators feel themselves well content. All students never were expected to be thus transformed.

In recent years there is a new attitude. Perhaps because of the growth of a developmental point of view in psychology and in the popular literatures, or because of the growth of an existential outlook stressing self-actualization, and certainly since the arrival of the personality psychologist on campus to study students not in terms of cognitive functioning but in terms of personality development, students—and their parents—now anticipate that in college they will change ipso facto. It has always been recognized that, when a young person leaves home—especially for the first long period of absence—that he will, on his return, be found somewhat altered. The scene at the rail or air terminal of the returning offspring being held at arm's length and inspected anxiously—"Let me see if you've changed?"—is very familiar.

Students have a much greater expectation of such today—not only of the possibility of change but of a virtual obligation to do so. In the progressive ideology of the day, change is good.

Some changes actively sought by many young students are similar to those defining positive growth according to the criteria of development-oriented personality psychologists. In general, the psychologist's stress is on expansion of the personality, a better differentiation of the parts, and a functioning that draws upon and integrates the various parts into a more complex and harmonious organization. Many of a person's resources are made available to him as a result of this development, and he is relatively freed from various internal constraints that prevent their flexible and appropriate use. On occasion attributes such as these can be isolated by young people and transformed into highly prized qualities. For example, in a recent high school newspaper, a young writer stresses in his article two qualities that are valued by contemporary youth— being concerned and being aware: "As DelValle students become more concerned with becoming concerned and more aware of the importance of becoming aware, their appreciation for such relevant assemblies as A.C.T.'s 'America—Black and White' also grows."

Often the quality or attitude that is prized and pursued becomes so reified that it is a thing unto itself—an entity apart from other experience. And a young person who perceives himself as having attained that prized quality may be unaware of his limited concept of it or himself. He may identify himself, for example, as a tolerant person. According to the current vogue, that means that he has empathic response to the situation of the poor, of racial minorities, and of young people who wish to live life unconventionally. But, whereas he may learn to express tolerance in this manner and according to these prescriptions, he nevertheless may be unable to see that he is essentially intolerant—of the establishment, of his parents, of middle-class values, of the police. He is defining tolerance in terms of specifics whereas genuine tolerance is an underlying trait.

The fact that change itself has become an ideal to pursue changes the study of change. It has been demonstrated already that the attitude and opinion scales may be approached with a new different attitude and perception of the items. Furthermore, students frequently respond to the current ideology by adopting it uncritically, by giving themselves and others the impression that they now are different; but this may be a very different sort of change from that conceived by the developmental psychologist or the liberal educator. The psychologist's expectation would be something perhaps best described "development of character."

The student adopting the current ideology is, in a sense, expressing himself in the form of a cliche. His tolerance is not so much a matter of inner conviction, based on experiences that have led him to believe that intolerance is fundamentally wrong; his tolerance is, rather, a conforming to the external standard—he is tolerant because tolerant is currently "the way to be." (In 1972, the impulse to change that springs from forced consciousness—a sense of obligation to conform to a sort of perpetual tribal *rite de passage*—can be seen reflected in attitudes toward sexual experience. There is a strong social expectation among contemporary youth suggesting that sexual intercourse is mandatory in order to be a member in good standing of some hypothetical but highly desirable youth culture. This emblematic necessity often means that old patterns are reversed: a couple, perforce, establishes intimacy at the physical level as a preliminary to getting to know each other in a more personal and all-encompassing way. Students often report such experiences to be physically unsatisfying; their satisfaction, apparently, comes from having done the proper thing according to the prevailing cultural definition.)

Under the pressure of student culture, a new student on campus may devote much attention—consciously or unconsciously —to emulating what he perceives the ideal college student to be. It may be said he dons an emblem of identity, a sort of college uniform, such as one exemplified by the traditional fraternity or sorority image. A more contemporary fashion of uniform, however, is that in college one is expected to change. In either case the uniform permits the student to engage in a pattern of new behaviors. Incidental to the newly permitted behaviors—or perhaps in response to them—there may be learning that represents a genuine personality change. On the other hand, it is possible that he uses the uniform to maintain an external facade behind which he remains essentially unchanged.

There is nothing novel about the phenomenon of self-conscious change. Persons in situations new to them almost always react by observing the manners and mores of the situation and make some effort to adapt. As Reisman (1950) notes, under such circumstances, the tendency is to other-directedness. However, the pattern of change of the student who is responding to the contemporary ideology of change often is an enduring one, carried on long after the necessity for adaptation to the new situation is over. There often is an amusing superficiality about the images adopted and, at the same time, a rather frightening sense of underlying desperation. A young person engaged in this kind of eager pursuit is an intellectual camp follower of contemporary student social fashion. As person, he seems often to have shrunk into insignificance: it is not he but an image that is important.

One student we observed is a young man who made a 180-degree change in appearance, behavior and attitude, but who nevertheless remained basically at the same developmental level. He entered the ECP in response to his parents' urging, but he left it before the end of the first semester: "I wasn't working very much. I decided that suddenly I would wake up and find I'd wasted all this time." He then considered going into psychology—his father's field—meanwhile speaking of "defining his own interests." From the first freshman year interview he was described, in part, as "lacking energy, enthusiasm, and interest. Sleeps after lunch."

By the middle of the sophomore year he seemed much changed: psychology now forgotten he decided that fraternity life and football—which attracted his interest after he left the Experimental Program—were not, after all, to his taste. At this point he described himself as a "person in change"; he said that he was reevaluating himself and that he valued himself for this reevaluation.

By the end of the junior year he was affecting a "hip" appearance: he wore a beard, talked and moved in a slow and leisurely manner. He spoke of being distant from the values of his mother "who tries to get me back to a safe middle-class life—straight through school, on to graduate school, and into a safe nine-to-five job." He expressed his determination to resist this pattern. He deplored his parents "control" of his brother. He said he had several LSD trips and felt they gave him some clear insight into himself. He was not sure that school was worth while. He had done well enough during the previous quarter but claimed that during the present quarter he was not studying. He was taking a course in art appreciation but claimed that he could see no relevance in it to himself.

The interviewer noted here that "his rejection of his old self and his parents' wishes for him is complete, and practically an opposite pole. He is leading a leisurely, bumming life absorbed with the new consciousness of himself."

At one level there was, indeed, a change but at another there was not. His behavior altered, but his personality structure essentially was the same as previously. The change was from compulsive conformity to compulsive rebellion. The compulsivity remained. He was concerned with the same matters and values—only in reverse. He was essentially the same person, as rigid as he was when he first entered college.

One of the young women in the Experimental Program was described as a "seducer" or a "bedazzler." Despite such descriptions, she remained aloof from personal involvements and seemed to be characterized by a similar quality of constant change. She changed in style of dress, in appearance, in her style of relating to others. She changed from a prototype of conventional Burbank to a Berkeley hippie, and back again. She elicited an uneasy feeling: who is this girl, when will she stop changing? A psychotherapist she consulted made the stringent observation that, for her, a real change might be indicated when *she* stopped changing—when she was able to be more stable in her presentation of self. This girl was among those students whom we judged, on the basis of our scales, not to have developed appreciably by the end of the second year.

Some students appear to follow a different pattern for dealing with the college experience. Rather than adopting whatever ideology, behavior, or manner of dress is presently in vogue, there is a tendency for the individual to remain essentially himself. In the process of living and working in college his personality becomes more sharply delineated—that is, he becomes less amorphous and more clearly differentiated—more complex and autonomous— holding on to his same basic values while changing some of his attitudes, opinions, and modes of behavior.

In contrast to the self-conscious sense of an obligation to change, there is a process of unself-conscious change for some students. Although such students may be aware of one or another popular image, they are not particularly interested in adopting it as a model. They are deeply immersed in their own activities. Change, for them, emerges naturally and unprovoked from the course of their involvement with their studies, projects, or nonacademic activities: while they are absorbed in learning or doing, their attitudes, interests, and behavior may gradually and unself-consciously alter, an alteration that is realized only when their involvement diminishes or their project is complete. In contrast to the more self-conscious students, these seem to be making changes in attitudes and points of view that are more subtle and more integral with the whole person.

A young man who struck us as having changed in an unself-conscious manner, declared—in an interview conducted in his junior year—that he felt he had not changed at all since he was a freshman in high school. He could discern no difference in his basic moral attitudes since age fourteen. His education, he said, had to do with facts and new perceptions arising from facts: for example, learning that great national heroes were essentially human with faults and foibles like everyone else or realizing what ghetto family life is like through the eyes of a person living it. He remained steadfast in planning to become a lawyer but was directing his interests in the field toward civil liberties. During his senior year the interviewer noted no change whatsoever in this student's career orientation, social attitudes, interests in sports, or relations with girls, family, or the university. "But he appears to wear it all with more ease. He is more poised and appears more tolerant." Indeed, compared with the perspective he indicated as a freshman, there were great changes. He was more obliging and aggressive. Nevertheless, he felt himself to be basically the same.

One young woman appeared to be a rather bored, sophisticated sorority girl. While maintaining this stereotyped conventionality, she accomplished a great deal. In her third year we were impressed by changes that were apparent to us, although she was not particularly aware of them. These changes were not in the content of what she talked to us about but in the depth of her awareness about her beliefs, her ideas, and her perceptions. Although she was still in the process of breaking away from her parents (a process impeded by her clinging to their standards through her sorority membership), she appeared more straightforward about her feelings, making and standing by her decisions, decisions that she made realistically in terms of her needs rather than by convention.

By taking extra units she was able to graduate a year early, still maintaining her B average. By selecting a social science field major she was able to take the courses in which she was interested: both social science and English. She was planning to marry upon graduation and to work; she was aware of the limitations in employment opportunities for women. Although the sorority had been useful to her, she was increasingly aware of the limited interests of the other girls; they were beginning to appear immature to her.

As a freshman she had begun to think about issues first stated by one of her professors, issues which centered about values associated with the hip movement and radical life style. Her thinking had been further stimulated by her brother, who had become a hippie, and by discussions with her parents, who opposed his new values. In the process of talking with them, she had come to know and appreciate her parents as individuals and to feel closer to them in a more adult way. When she took a second course from the professor who had first stated the issues, she found his new ideas no longer struck her as original because she had already come to them in the process of her own thinking.

At the end of the third year she impressed her interviewer as a sensible, level-headed, practical young woman who had used various aspects of the university to help herself in her thinking rather than simply as a means to earn certification and who, in the process, had become more fully herself.

A change from a rather conservative to a relativistic point of view was made by a young man in the ECP. John was rather cynical and self-denigrating at the outset. Over all four years these attitudes altered. On our personality measures his profile changed from a suggestion of tightness and counterphobic self-assertiveness to a comfortable stance which allowed him to see the world less in terms of black and white. He made a fair, but mixed impression on his first teacher: "Bright, quick, mercurial fellow, who has capacity to do first-rate work. One of his papers was excellent. Unfortunately he has a tendency to perform, to clown his way from important, personal, and, perhaps, painful discussion to safer, less important banter. He has a good mind which he apparently lacks confidence in. Or he lacks confidence in some facet of his character. Nevertheless, he appears to have much to offer. The hope is that when he can begin to appreciate his own true worth he will no longer find it necessary to do a soft shoe routine instead of earnestly entering into serious conversation. We feel that he has the potential to become one of the better students in the program."

It is interesting that this evaluation noted a discrepancy between ability and achievement, for it was a similar evaluation, based on an IQ test and his high school performance, that John felt led to his reluctance to perform in school. He was actively interested in history, and he read a great deal in high school, yet he so resented school work—which he regarded as busy work—that he "fudged through" with C's. He was admitted to Berkeley on a conditional basis, under the sponsorship of a professor who knew his family.

Coming to the university apparently was not a strain for him. He enjoyed a weekly round of golf with his professor friend, joined a fraternity (and once was jailed over a prank), and he did not work any harder than he did in high school. Having lived and traveled in other parts of the world, he had acquired sophistication. He was conventional and conservative in his views: one professor noted that John favored rigid law and order and supported the Vietnam war.

Also, it was apparent that John was a game player who devoted himself to making a good impression and getting grades by putting forth the least possible effort. In one of his first-semester papers he attempted to impress his teacher as he was accustomed to do in high school. As he saw it later, the act was "a sophomoric effort to compare a Greek play to a soap opera, as a dodge to cover up my lack of understanding." His teacher, who already was aware of a covert but pervasive cynicism in his manner, told him forthrightly that he thought the paper was fraudulent. John responded to this criticism with some indication that he way enjoying his own cleverness. He assured us and apparently himself, that he really wanted to do well. He then began his reading early, read and reread material he was neglecting, and underlined important passages. But his performance did not improve, and consequently he was very discouraged at the end of the first semester.

As he continued trying to become a serious student, John became involved in the intellectual work of the program. With involvement, a conflict developed between his intellectual interests and his commitment to the military. Because of his familiarity with military life (his father was a career officer), and for expedient reasons of income and the draft, he was signed up for the reserve officer training program on campus. In the first year he began feeling that military training was contradictory to his intellectual work and growth. Later he said, "It is ironic that military science alienated me because I agreed with many of their tenets. . . . But, as far as they are concerned, you must support a given policy because you are ordered to do so." He perceived a sharp contrast between total control in the military program and the Experimental College Program, where he felt encouraged to develop his own thinking and point of view. The contrast was epitomized by moving from twice-weekly, exhausting and relentlessly executed military drills to the informality and flexibility of seminar discussions in the ECP. It was always a difficult transition, and sometimes he felt it was impossible. At the end of the first year he resigned from the reserve program. He completed the ECP satisfactorily and continued his academic work through the remaining two years of college without special event.

In our discussion group at the end of the senior year he was one of the most thoughtful people we encountered. He was enjoying his life, not as "fun," but as hard work in exploring, learning, and changing. In predicting what our study would learn about change in college, John felt major changes would take place in the first two years:

You will find a point of extreme cynicism and iconoclasm, because when you come here you find everything you believe in is wrong—that causes a reaction—and you move away from that reaction of cynicism as time progresses because you find things here a person can believe in. For myself, I understand the outside society more but I can relate to it less, live in it less.

I've evolved a personal philosophy, of how I want to live my life—and that doesn't mix with the rest of the society—not compatible too much—but then, I don't believe my answer is everybody else's answer.

When I came here, everything I had accepted was gradually

torn down. I had to build my own personal philosophy—especially be-
cause Berkeley is so political—in order to relate to Berkeley politics.
Berkeley politics is a very compelling thing. I had to figure myself
out first—I evolved through a lot of changes, my own feeling about
power and about human relations—which I feel is the basis of my
personal philosophy, which is that one should have as few con-
straints as possible placed on the expression of your total, of yourself.
And the culture, your cultural tradition, limits you, very much. And
if you are a little bit credulous and a little bit willing to accept
strange things, then you can experience a whole range of things that
you would not—that your culture would not—allow you to experi-
ence. That's sort of where I got and that makes me kind of an
anarchist politically.

When someone in the group asked what he thought contributed to the development of his philosophy, John's answer indicated that he had a strong sense of independence:

Everything was important. The iconoclasm, people not ac-
cepting, questioning value systems. A complete reversal of any
school experiences I've ever had, immediately upon my arrival. I
was expelled from high school, in trouble all the way through, just
got C's and everything. I talked my way into school, into the Tuss-
man program. All of a sudden everything was different. I was
relating to what was happening, and people were trying to be honest
with each other. I don't know that they really were necessarily, but
they were trying. I don't think I had ever been in a situation where
people were really trying to be honest with each other. They really
questioned things. That's the way it was on that level. And on
another level, smoking grass, getting turned on to the drug scene,
which makes you so all of a sudden look at your whole society, your
whole context, in a completely different—from a different stand-
point. (Because of the grass?) Oh, yeah, and everything. The whole
Berkeley experience. It's hard to pick out any one thing and say
that's the most significant thing. This place is very heavy.

Experiencing the "Berkeley scene" was emphasized by many
students in their efforts to understand what was especially meaning-

ful to them during college. Some others in the group agreed with John that simply being exposed to the "scene" was important to them, too. John explained that he meant a sense of assimilating the exposure in an open-minded manner. He observed that he and others in the ROTC program did not relate to the university at all, at the beginning. They were cut off completely. Only when they began relating to the Berkeley community and trying to get involved in it did many basic changes begin to occur. Another student, a young woman in the group, objected that she could not see how anybody could come to Berkeley and be "cut off" completely: "If you're here, you're exposed to it—if you just walk down Telegraph Avenue." He replied, "But that doesn't mean you relate to it. A lot of people here don't relate to it. They don't want to understand it and just block it all out."

The distinction between being *exposed* to, and *relating* to is one John considered important. In the following exchange with one of the other women in the group he made it even more clear that he was aware that a person is essentially the one who is responsible for his life being the way it is. Apparently responding to his note of adventure and enjoyment, she asked him how he developed such a positive attitude about all of his experience. He didn't know. He said he simply liked it here and liked the people. In her experience, the woman said she felt she was directed; she had a sense that her life decisions were being made for her by social institutions (a sense of life that many students expressed and many, today, still do). She said, "I know I direct myself, but seeing how a system tells you . . . you are taught something and you use it to your own end. I'm in the Peace Corps and going to grad school. Okay. You may be able to use it, but at the same time you are being used as a resource. I don't want to be just used as a resource." By being in the Peace Corps, she felt that someone was getting something out of her and so hindering her, limiting her own interests, and keeping her from being free.

He responded, "That depends very much on where your head is at. Whether you are willing to let. . . . Like, I accept that there has to be a society, and studying history and anthropology, I've come to the unshakeable conclusion that all societies are screwed up and its ridiculous to say that one society is, that *your* society is not going to be screwed up, because it *is*. It just could be less screwed up than other societies, and, but, you have to have societies, especially now, because you have all these—social structure, technological structure, and industrial complex—and it supports more people than the ground would if it all fell down. And all these constraints that society puts on you also keep people living together and keep them alive, and, you know, there have been few societies that have done that at all well. And so, okay, so I don't mind coping with society, and I don't feel like—if society uses me, I'll contribute something and I think it's all according to where my head's at, whether it's a big heavy thing or not, and I don't think it's a big, heavy thing."

Although he referred to himself as an anarchist, John's point of view clearly was still basically conservative, but was enlightened, not rigid, conservatism. In discussing the campus atmosphere he said: "I loved the university the first two years because I thought they were so nice, because they let me in, they did all kinds of things, they didn't hassle me, they weren't going to kick me out because I talked in class and things like that. Meanwhile, the kids, the rallies and stuff, were just as dogmatic as the people I knew in the South, and they really put me off, so I didn't relate. . . . It's a very scary thing, because they make the same kind of moral judgments about other people in the plaza as the College of Cardinals does. That's what's *wrong* with society: people making judgments about other people's morality. 'I don't have to reason with you any more because if you think that, then you are immoral. . . . I can use all these sanctions.' "

Many students believe that drug use gives them freedom from the constraints of society. Others feel that it provides new experiences, greater awareness, and expands their minds. In a discussion of this kind, John expressed another view:

I think one thing that it really does to a person is kind of structure your relationship to your society. All of a sudden you're looking at society from the other side of the law. It's a very freaky thing. Like, you know, you see that, you begin to realize that, "My God!" There really are things that in terms of individuals are really

*bummers, that you just didn't think were at all, that you didn't
really relate to. You didn't see how you can't relate to somebody
being executed by the state unless you can relate to, you know, put
yourself in that position. And being on the other side of the society,
feeling that society is going to come after you, that society, for
doing something you're doing, society can, you know, incarcerate
you or do whatever they want with you. I think it becomes a very
important—significant—realization to people that, you know, all of
a sudden you realize that this thing, this whole system that you live
in, can devour you. But at the same time also that, you know, like
I began to look at other societies in those terms too. What would it
be like? What would they bust me for in Nazi Germany? What
would they bust me for in medieval Islam? What would they bust
me for a Brazil?*

Upon graduation John was considering joining the Peace
Corps. He wished to return to Malaysia, where he spent part of his
adolescence, and to help the Malaysian people develop their crop
yields—after he learned how to do it himself. The idea was not
merely to improve their food supply but to produce a surplus that
could be sold to gain the power that the big powers respect: money.
This pragmatic attitude, the acceptance of the broad relationship of
things to each other, seemed a far cry from the tightly organized
young man who, in his first semester, could not let himself consider
anything seriously. I am not suggesting that all his experiences were
positive or that all his actions were necessarily integrative but that,
on the whole, he seemed to use college experiences toward his development. As we completed our report during the year following
graduation, we learned that he apparently was carrying out his
intentions; he was a graduate student in Asian studies.

The story of this young man is a variation on a common
theme, in its most general form the theme of liberalization or of
liberation: the development of a young person who begins college
relatively constrained and oriented to authority and ends four years
later oriented to his own judgment, flexible, and relativistic in his
views. Instead of struggling with himself and authority he was
working more or less effectively for himself.

Some students are even more contained at the outset than

John. These account for the entering freshman described as "having an authoritarian attitude." Such young people arrive in college with considerable uncertainty about themselves and their power, and they look for external guides: the expectations of their teacher (what does he want me to know?), the certainty of facts about the world, and the truth in all matters. These young people, in a sense, are not fully integrated. They must discover themselves by realizing that there are no final answers and no authorities they can depend on absolutely.

Many do get a definition of themselves and their own power in this way, not usually consciously. Such a definition is often implicit in their discussions about themselves. They speak of having experienced a shift from feeling unsure about their opinions and being impressed with the certitude of facts and the wisdom of their teachers to feeling confident about their opinions and viewing the world in less absolute terms.

Some experience the shift in only a limited way. Others foreclose the possibility of such a shift by committing themselves to one or another form of dogma. For example, several students we knew became strongly engaged in religious movements. Some became dedicated to proselytizing fellow students to join also. For the most part, they were engaged in well-known fundamentalist religions. However, we included among these students one who became dedicated to Scientology and intended to become an official in that organization and two whose total commitment to encounter group work—both as participants and later as leaders—impressed us as comparable to a conversion to religious belief. No doubt there are other variations on this theme, such as particular philosophical points of view or scientific theories becoming absolute dogma to young persons seeking certainty.

Young persons become interested in religious philosophies for more reasons than uncertainty. Some of our students at the end of their fourth year did appear firmly and dogmatically committed. We knew others, however, who intensively explored a particular religion or sometimes several, but their interest in something sure seemed transient; even while we still knew them they proceeded to other interests.

One young woman appeared to have a different reason for

her interest in religion. She became acquainted with it through her academic studies, personally and also as an ideal commitment to serving community well-being. Unlike the others, who were uncertain of themselves and afraid to act, she felt a readiness to act that she feared might lead her to overdo and become overinvolved. Sarah was a substitute for a student who left college and therefore was first interviewed in the middle of the second year. She was described as "tall, large girl, reddish hair, angular. Glasses. In jumper. Neat looking. Gives precise answers, has opinions on everything." Her sense of energy, of self-assurance, and readiness to act was apparent immediately. Also apparent was her awareness of these qualities in herself and her need to restrain them. When asked to tell about experiences that were most important to her since coming to Berkeley, she immediately responded, "My involvement in politics." She had been involved in civil rights activity in the East and had moved toward the left. She said: "I have to keep in mind the complexity and not get involved in black and white foolishness that goes on with radicals on this campus." She worked full time on the student strike her first year at Berkeley. She said: "Someday we are going to get the things we strike for, preferably not in the way used in the strike. But there is no stop to it."

Her parents were conservative, graduates of eastern colleges, and they sent her to a private high school. Both parents worked. They were not active in the community politically or socially, though they adhered to conventional social codes and wanted her to enter society formally with a debut, which she refused. Of her relationship to them she said: "I don't feel I am rebelling; I just don't feel related to them. I just don't talk to them if there is a conflict." Sarah thought her family had little to offer: "They're hung up on background—old New England; that's about all they have left." Her father was painfully shy and unassertive. Her mother gave up her intellectual interests for marriage but "can be pretty reasonable."

Sarah felt she did not know how to handle social situations. She was particularly shy with men, and much of her social experience was in the context of work parties, political action groups, and so on. She was very active with groups but did not join them. She rejected homosexual relationships (to which she was exposed in high school). She felt herself to be intellectually arrogant but tending to balanced thinking. She majored in history as she decided in the eighth grade and planned to teach at the college level. Her leisure reading was mostly nonfiction, including modern Christian theology and current events. She already was a dedicated scholar.

The theme of self-control was prominent in her talks with us. She smoked marijuana—"like social drinking." She would not take LSD because of disturbed periods in high school when she had a "tendency to go in myself, to wish to take something that takes me inside." It was as though she felt her impulsive energies were precariously balanced and she feared going too far outside or inside herself. She felt a temptation of this sort in the political activity in Berkeley and deliberately returned each summer to the extreme conservatism of a New England summer camp for adolescents where she was a counselor and taught mountain climbing. She said it served as a balance to the radical, oversimplified position taken on campus—a position toward which she felt herself impelled—as well as to the generally free and open attitudes stressed in Berkeley living. It also may have served to bridge the gap with home. "The camp is a good environment; it does good things in a close situation. It helps develop my tolerance for incongruity. Each change back and forth is a cultural shock, but I can still talk to those people." In her work she felt she could give the children a feeling that it was possible not to be confused by the multiplicity of environments in the technological world. "Mountain climbing is a character-building exercise. Character is built through exercise, and discomfort is good for you. Self-restraint is good for you. You learn the ropes, and then you know what you ought to be doing. You can throw yourself into things with exorbitant emotion. It's the joy of survival and doing well." As she talked about Berkeley and the camp, it seemed that she feared she might settle for one of them so she made herself learn to live in both environments.

At the end of the second year Sarah said she was having more unintellectual fun in her house with "grass pushers" living below and lots of people going in and out. She was high quite often. She had a boyfriend but thought the relationship was not important because she was not afraid of him and if something really touched her she would be afraid. However, she found out that men were human.

Even in her intellectual efforts she was acutely aware of the balance between her impulse to plunge into the world or out of it. She was writing a paper on Henry Adams. She felt somehow related to him in her emphasis on order and rationality and because of her aristocratic background. She thought it was not good for her to think of herself as an anachronism brought up with values that no longer existed. She might find it easy to think the world was going to the dogs and look on it from the outside.

In her third year a change in feelings about herself began to take place, although the change was not apparent until toward the end of the fourth year. Her activities at Berkeley, both political and social, began to be somewhat frenetic, even as her interest in them began to concern her and to diminish. At the same time, her feelings toward her parents and about her activities on the East Coast became less ambivalent. She had enjoyed her work in the summer camp, looked forward to the following summer, and her visit home at Christmas was less of an ordeal for her.

She was engaged in many activities during that third year at Berkeley: demonstrations at the Oakland Induction Center, participation in several campus ad hoc political groups, speeches at illegal rallies. She was not enthusiastic in these activities but, dutifully, felt they needed her support.

Her social activities increased and involved greater intimacy, stimulation, and expression of feeling than before. She shared her apartment with several young men and women. The door was open, many of their friends were frequent informal visitors, and she found herself fascinated to hear gossip about many individuals but also somewhat overwhelmed and confused by the intimate view of people it afforded her.

A young man who was a year behind her in school but who also was majoring in history became her focus of interest. She enjoyed her relationship with him because—unlike prior relationships with men—it was not intellectual. They slept and played together. The experience was exciting in itself, and it pleased her to be personally free to do it.

During the year she felt herself to be less intellectually aggressive, less inclined to expound ideas to her friends, less the completely predictable, efficient, intellectual young woman she had been. She saw herself becoming hedonistic, like the others around her. She took LSD once during the year. At the same time Sarah was excited by her free way of life. She also was concerned she might become too carefree; already she was aware of ignoring other people and overlooking her roommate's feelings. She felt she lacked a commitment to something. During the winter her studies of metaphysics led her to consider becoming a Christian. She had nobody understanding to talk with about this phase of her life, but the idea remained in her thoughts. In spite of her pleasure in life she felt she wanted a higher cause or belief to inspire and guide her, a cause beyond rationality.

In her senior year the pattern of change continued. Although she was still active politically, it was out of a sense of duty and altruism. Although still involved with her boyfriend, their relationship lacked the former spirit of spontaneity. Although still willing to take an LSD trip with her roommate "so that I can understand her symbols," she felt disenchanted with the idea. By this time the Berkeley atmosphere, with its emphasis on politics, drugs, and unbridled expression of feeling, seemed dismal to her.

Instead Sarah found satisfaction in her academic work. She had continued her study of religions, and in a history honors program she became engaged in writing a thesis on Victorian religions. She was a fine scholar and enjoyed her work, which offered both a sense of discovery and excitement and order.

At the end of the year a young woman, Lynn, spoke in the discussion group about finding the greatest fulfillment and the most personal effectiveness in building the revolution. She was speaking of the revolution which she perceived beginning in America against established institutions and values. She made the point that her personal desires were quite compatible with the essence of the revolutionary movement, so they would not be squelched in her work in that movement.

DEBBY: *That's really interesting because when I first came here I was involved in a Zionist movement, and I had very altruistic, idealistic feelings, and then gradually I got away from that and started to care more about myself and what I wanted to do, individually.*

SARAH: *I think both those things have happened to me at once. If I were to pinpoint what it is that makes that true it's that in the last year I've become a Christian. That makes me a great deal more committed to my radicalness. It also makes me very much responsible for everything I do so that it's both those things happening at once.*

DEBBY: *Was this sort of a mystical experience? Rational?*

SARAH: *No, it's not at all mystical. It was a rational experience and one that surprised me to death. But there I was . . . almost an academic experience.*

DEBBY: *Did this, like, environment not force you into it but heavily influence you into that decision?*

SARAH: *No. This environment had very little to do with it. As a matter of fact, I had, I—what precipitated it?—a lot of study on my own of. . . . I'm in history and I'm very heavy into history and I've studied what causes change and I've studied what are the dynamics of change at any time; effectively, that's what history is. And looking at it long enough I ended up a Christian and that means a lot of study of the Middle Ages and also means a lot of study of right now. And I've always been more or less politically active. I'm much more committed now. Before I was active; now I'm committed because there's a much stronger guiding factor overriding the whole thing.*

DEBBY: *That's really interesting. That's about the first thing I've heard of like that. Did you come from a Christian family?*

SARAH: *Yeah, but I. . . . No, there was not much pressure, and I was, you know, a good militant atheist in high school. I suppose there was some sort of backlash when I was doing it. I would definitely say there was backlash when I was doing it. It was somewhat neurotic.*

DEBBY: *Do you think it's political now or is it really religious with you?*

SARAH: *It's religious.*

DEBBY: *That's really interesting.*

SARAH: *I consider myself a freak, you know. I do find myself a freak. I also like school and that makes me an incredible freak among people that I associate with. I don't say that they have to like school and I don't say that school does anything for them, but I've discovered how to make something out of it by pushing and pulling and insisting on doing it on my own and that sort of thing. And that works. I think that's something everybody's run into.*

DEBBY: *Are you doing anything with a group? The "Christian whatever"?*

SARAH: *No. I'm not doing anything with anybody as far as that's concerned.*

DEBBY: *So, it's all on your own.*

SARAH: *Yeah.*

GROUP LEADER: *Why does that lead to a greater commitment?*

SARAH: *I have more responsibilities all over the place; I have more responsibility to worry since we happen to be in this theoretical democracy and therefore we're theoretically supposed to be interested. I have more responsibility to attempt to carry out that in such a way as to make the thing work (which at this point I completely agree with Lynn's requirements for a revolution—I'm not quite sure exactly what kind, but you've got to have a revolution in order to do that) so I have more responsibility to do that. I can't put that in to try and keep my, you know, to do what I need to do for my own head to do that right; and I also have a responsibility to be committed to making this a more possible community; it's not even a possible community at the moment.*

This student's intellectual interests and scholarship had for some time provided a framework, order, and meaning for her life such that her dilemmas regarding sexual and social impulses were manageable. Becoming a Christian (sparked, in part, by her reading of Teilhard de Chardin's sweeping concept of God) apparently provided something more: an integration of disparate, conflicting elements in herself, which gave unity to her intellectual and social interests and direction and meaning to all her actions. It did not appear to be a foreclosure but was a new guiding philosophy, although we suspected that her humor, particularly about herself, might be giving way to what seemed awesome seriousness. She felt *change* was the wrong word for what happened to her. "I haven't changed, I have become more so. I see things as a continuity." She went on to do graduate work at Harvard.

There were other students dealing with a similar developmental problem—those who came to college relatively self-confident; they were talented people with greater than usual readiness to act on their impulses and to act independently. Some of our observations suggest that more young men and women coming to college are like this (Chapter Seven) and that there are many variations on this theme. As in the case of the student just described, their impulsivity may threaten them; or, it may involve them in diffuse activity with no direction, as with the student who constantly changes. It may make it difficult for them to function productively in the academic setting or in their personal relationships. At a deeper level they may have a painful time dealing with their rages and their tenderness.

A student of this sort may be regarded in a different way from the student looking for an external authority. This relatively more impulsive type often may be seen as a revolutionary trying to change his world to suit his views. I am describing an interpersonal "revolutionary" who tries to make every relationship or personal situation suit himself: an operator, a person who attempts to manipulate, charm, or bedevil those with whom he comes in contact. Typically, he "gets away with murder." Because of his talent at charming, he never quite has to meet the requirements and therefore never fully engages himself in anything. He has never realized himself, his power, or his capacity. To do so, he has to be able to choose to do something in the world rather than simply changing situations to suit himself. He has to come up against someone who will not be charmed or manipulated or will not let him get away with it.

Such a young person often is among those who most frequently drop out of college. Or he may, because he is talented, charm his way through college, always with special arrangements and accommodations. He may find himself through personal encounter with a teacher—sometimes with a psychotherapist—or through a demanding intellectual interest and commitment which provides some integration, as it did for the young woman just described.

These are some of the variations on the theme of change in college. Sometimes there is only an appearance of change, but most individuals I have described in some detail represent in one degree or another good developmental change, with the individual able to make a life for himself and apparently still in the process of change as he leaves the university.

There are a myriad of other outcomes. Some students, those who fall by the wayside, seem worse off for their experiences, some permanently—committing suicide, experiencing profound psychiatric illness—some temporarily—experiencing transient psychiatric or physical illness, dropping out, or changing goals and plans because of external events, such as military service.

In brief, various changes take place as the students deal or fail to deal with the problems and situations with which the college presents them and into which their interests lead them. Rapid social change is altering attitudes about change and the study of it. Rapid social change, particularly to the extent that it contains an ideology that stresses the importance of change, modifies the interaction between the person who is the subject of study and the instrument used to study him. Such change also modifies the interaction of the person and his natural inclination toward development because that development is forced, in many instances, into a more conscious process than it usually has been in past generations. Thus, some of our subjects are more centrally caught up with the process itself than are others who continue, in traditional fashion, to let the development happen while they go about their business in college.

A final thought regarding the nature of developmental change. Of the two general patterns we observed, un-self-conscious change seemed to relate more to the essence of the person than did changes which were consciously adopted. Basic personality change can be achieved by means of deliberately chosen action (Wheelis, 1969; Mead, 1964). Perhaps, however, the individuals we observed—those caught up in the fashion of having to have an image or definition of self different from the one with which they came to college—were extreme examples of self-conscious change.

In the case of the pattern of change that involves less self-conscious effort, a challenge stimulating change may be encountered in the form of an intolerable discrepancy (such as ROTC drill versus Experimental College seminars) or a challenge sought out (as smoking pot in Berkeley and doing character-building in New England). Whatever the challenge, the basic context in which it is encountered, it would appear, must be one of engagement: as John said, it is not just a matter of exposure but a matter of relating.

Chapter 11

Reflections

*T*his first attempt to develop an Experimental College Program was both a success and a failure. It provided a unique atmosphere and academic structure in which some students developed in different ways from students in the regular lower division program. But on the other hand, it appeared to the faculty that little happened as was intended; it appeared that the plan was not working and that they were making the best of an impossible situation and seeing it through—sometimes by makeshift means—to the end of the second year.

What went wrong? Why didn't it work? For one thing, teaching experience over previous years had not prepared the faculty for the new student who appeared unexpectedly on the scene with heretofore unheard of or at least unusual characteristics that seemed, at times, to typify an entire group of students. The basic cultural change had just emerged as an actuality in the form of the Free Speech Movement (Chapter Seven). Prior expressions of the new student qualities were isolated, unitary, events—the student protest of the House Un-American Activities Committee at the San Francisco City Hall, four years prior to the Free Speech Movement—or they were manifested only in individual actions, such as going into the South to work in the civil rights movement. For another thing, the self-selection of volunteers for the Experimental College Program emphasized some personality qualities prominent in the "new student" (Chapter Three): a greater sense of autonomy and a readiness to act on impulse, together with an almost programmatic stance against authoritarian attitudes. Some of these students, free from constraints of the regular undergraduate program, became "activist" in the program, demanding a voice in its administration and behaving unilaterally in regard to academic requirements. The teaching assistants also had the new student qualities and strongly asserted their interests. Although there were many positive and rewarding experiences for students, teaching assistants, and faculty, there were periods—especially in the first year—of great abrasiveness between them.

The faculty—like many other faculties since then—were, as a group, unprepared to deal with these student qualities in the program. Equally as important was the fact that they were unprepared to deal with each other. They were five individuals working together for the first time: intensely individualistic persons accustomed to emphasize their personal uniqueness as teachers within the confines of their own classrooms. In the program, however, although individuality was certainly not discouraged, they were expected to work together—to teach the same curriculum at the same time and to emphasize the same themes. Personal styles, personal tastes, and personal paces needed to be coordinated. Obviously, it was a task that would take some time to accomplish.

Indeed, there is a serious question as to whether it could be accomplished at all by such a faculty from such a campus. Several factors are important. A faculty attracted to a prominent university which provides prestige in the academic world tends to be a group self-selected in terms of certain particular qualities. These no doubt include a desire to hold a prestigious position. Generally speaking, such a desire also implies a need for traditional social structures which underlie and define such a position. Furthermore, given the traditional route by which one enters university teaching—from college to graduate school and thence to the teaching appointment —many of these men were never really outside the academic structure in their entire lives. As a result, they probably were men who intellectually conceived the ideal of an "open" educational structure but were emotionally unprepared to live in one.

Tussman's greatest problem in this and subsequent attempts to initiate the ECP was one of recruiting faculty from the Berkeley campus, a fact that is in accord with the view I am here proposing. In his second effort to carry out the program (1967–1969) the entire faculty was recruited from other less prestigious colleges and universities. (And it is of some interest that the second attempt was much more harmonious for the faculty than was the first, in spite of student qualities similar to those of the first group of students.)

The ostensible reason for this recruiting problem was faculty reluctance to interrupt—for a period of two years—departmental connections and work which was in the context of and dedicated to career advancement. Remaining in a structure representing permanence was a primary concern and one that would make it difficult to change to a more open work situation, especially one with a limited career future.

Finally, it is necessary to take into account Tussman's own structural situation in the first attempt to develop the experimental program. His situation (and also that of the rest of the faculty) involved developing a program intended to be a separate entity, counterposed to the lower division program. Inevitably, this situation put the faculty in a position of proving that the Experimental College Program could work. "I *must* make a success of it" was almost certainly in the background as each difficulty, conflict, and disagreement was encountered—thereby making it less possible dispassionately and calmly to consider problems introduced by unanticipated factors and to counter them with appropriate changes and adjustments. All reactions and anxieties, of course, were intensified in the Free Speech Movement climate of struggle over control.

These are important considerations for new programs, particularly those programs that attempt to provide new structures for faculty, and faculty and students, to work together in such a way that the development of the individual student is a central educational consideration.

At this point a distinction should be made between the idea of a program and of educational innovations. Much is heard and read today of curricular and educational innovations. Study of some of these—both in my college system and in others across the country—leads me to believe that there are more revisions than innovations. For example, many so-called curricular innovations involve the same curriculum divided into units which permit the student to pursue his acquisition of information at his own pace, thereby making it possible for the rapid learner to move ahead faster and the slow learner—or the student also engaged in making a living—not to be unduly pressed by the arbitrary timing of the semester system. In this plan the student takes an examination in the subject when he is ready. The only innovation is in terms of individualization of the pace of work. The curriculum is the same.

More far-reaching innovations emphasize community. Students live and sometimes work together and are associated with the same faculty over some period in their college career. Although a personalization of their experience in this plan is possible, and, with it a sense of unity and coherence, the curriculum still remains essentially the same. It is arranged in courses according to tradition, departmental territorial rights, administrative convenience, and similar considerations. The curriculum has little more unity and coherence than in the traditional arrangement.

I believe that the ECP is a more comprehensive program which is truly new in all fundamental respects. I would define the program as concerned with providing a community in which personal experience—especially of student with teacher—enhances the learning process and allows full attention to the intellectual process and to the intellectual development of the individual student, his style of work, and his pace, as well as a curriculum that in its organization provides a sense of unity and wholeness. The latter may be attained with a required curriculum planned in terms of basic questions or meanings—as in the ECP—or it may be attained by carefully relating the areas of study to the intellectual development of the student, as in an alternate major in psychology now being developed by some colleagues and me at California State University, San Francisco.

To return to considerations arising from our study of the ECP, regarding these kinds of programs, it is clear that an intellectual commitment to an "open" plan or a "community of learners" is not enough to consider. If it is to achieve such a community, the faculty must tolerate the new and unexpected, for, in any circumstance which permits relationships to develop and grow, the unanticipated paradoxically is inevitable. By tolerance I mean more than a realization that events and problems will emerge: a readiness to accept them and to adapt them to serve the purposes of the program. The Experimental College Program, for example, might have prospered had the faculty been able to relate their collegial problems and their problems with student demands to the overall curriculum. To use their own problems in living together and their efforts at resolution of those problems as an empirical case in point of the curricular themes may not have been easy, but, if successful, it might have made the program more engaging and the curriculum more meaningful than it was. Certainly nothing has more relevance than one's own experience.

The position of the program vis-a-vis the academic community as a whole is another important consideration. Both the attitude of the university community to the special program and the attitude the program faculty holds are important. The central issue here is how the program is regarded. It may be considered as an experiment in the trial of a new idea—a pilot study attempting to learn whether some action is feasible and what problems are involved, whether the idea works, how it works, and whether it is something worth repeating. In such a trial nothing is "on trial." It is essentially an exploration. In another view, the experiment is an experiment as a test. The program is thought of as being compared with an alternative way of doing the same thing as the ECP, for example, was compared with the regular lower division program. This kind of trial poses the question, does it work?, or, does it work as well as or better than the regular program? If the participants consider it a better way of doing things or have some other investment in the idea, the question easily becomes an imperative, that is, it *must* work. In this view, there is a fundamental tension that may have a limiting, constricting effect—particularly in response to an unexpected turn of events—while the tension of the former view, which is related to the excitement of trying out something new, may be liberating. The unexpected will be viewed with curiosity and interest in the first instance and with apprehension and efforts at control in the second.

Another consideration regards the relationship of the program and the larger academic community: should the special program be protected from the influence of the degree-granting program which is simultaneously carried on in the larger university community? A program oriented to development of the individual student, in order to achieve its goal, must be free of the pressures that prevail in a degree granting program, that is, pressures to produce work that will earn the highest possible credit in a fixed period of time and in competition with other students (such competition often artificially reinforced by the use of the normal curve as a basis for assigning the distribution of grades within the context of a given class).

Students considering the special program often imply such pressure in their question, "Will this program prepare me for advanced (or for graduate) work?" An influence also is implicit in faculty responsibility to "translate" work evaluations in the special program into the language (credits and grades) of the standard college transcript. Concern about these kinds of pressures in the Experimental College Program was expressed by the fact that potential physical science majors were warned that they could not be prepared for such a major in the program. Also, students in the program were urged to use their one outside course each semester to satisfy the university language requirement so they would not be burdened with it in their upper division work. Ideally, the outside course (necessary, incidentally, so that the student in the program could earn proper credit in his first two years for entry into his third year at the university) could have been used to add depth to themes emerging in response to the special program curriculum.

A final consideration regarding the program and the larger community concerns the teacher's freedom to innovate. There is evidence in the problems of recruitment at Berkeley that career

considerations and the conventional structure of the university—
schools and departments within which careers must be advanced—
tend to limit the initiation and development of new programs, without regard to administrative structures and procedures which usually
are maintained in status quo, and which, therefore, have an inertia
antithetical to the introduction of new procedures.

If we are to have the experimental programs we seem to need
so desperately, the structure of the university, the school, the division, the department, and especially those men and women who are
administratively responsible for those structures, must provide—as
a structural and administrative necessity—a regular place for new
programs. Teachers must have not only opportunity, cooperation,
and support but active protection from the influence and pressures
of existing structures and programs. Faculty should be able to offer
programs for varying periods of time according to their interests and
the students' interests and needs. An emphasis on continuing experimentation with new educational forms would provide a means
whereby higher education and rapid cultural change could be integrated meaningfully in the student's life rather than being a source
of conflict, as it has for the most part been since 1965.

What are positive aspects of the Experimental College Program? What made the program work? The curriculum itself, of
course, was the thematic thread of the processes experienced in the
program. The exploration and elaboration of the curriculum by the
students with the help of their teachers provided an exciting view of
the world and of mankind. Students were free to use varied forms
of response to the curriculum in addition to participating in a seminar or writing an assigned essay. Having defined his particular interest in the area of study, a student could employ any of various
forms—a poem, a play, or an allegorical story—to express his ideas
about the subject. These alternatives also added to the challenge
and the stimulus of the program.

The fact that students spent—or could spend—most of their
working time (and social time, if they chose) together, producing
a sense of group identity, intensified their experiences of Berkeley, of
the university and of the Experimental College Program. Their
solidarity as a large student body group as well as their membership

and identity with one of the subgroups that formed within the program, provided many with a highly personal context in which their experiences were shared and integrated.

The process of evaluating the student's work had a most crucial effect on the positive outcome of the program. In the process of an individual critique of the student's work, taking place in a one-to-one tutorial, the teacher was able to know an individual very well. The teacher's observations of the student's work could be extensively explored, thus expanding both teacher's and student's understanding of the student's level of intellectual development. During a semester series of such meetings it was possible for the teacher to be concerned with the student as a whole person and to know him well enough to help him with his overall development. In some instances student and teacher worked together longer than one semester, thereby adding to the experience.

To varying degrees, students used these consultative relationships (designed for academic purposes, to review the student's intellectual functioning and encourage its development) for exploration of and decision-making about personal matters. Some such matters, far removed from educational considerations, could be seen, nevertheless, as related to the student's education. Generally, our educational procedures, to the extent that they do not make possible a personal relationship, do not allow a view of the whole person in this way. Moreover, because of the fact that in some instances we knew a student in both the educational and clinical settings at the same time, it was possible for us to see that the student was thinking about identical personally important matters at two different levels in the two situations. For example, a student in her seminar on Greek civilization was writing an imaginary play in which the Greek gods—engaged with each other in their own rivalries and passions—were the cause of events plaguing man on earth. At the same time, in talking with her therapist, she expressed concern about the effect on her and her younger brother of her parents' conflicts with each other. She seemed unaware of the relationship of the two levels and the fact that she was using both situations, in part, to think about the same personal matter—but it was evident to us.

Personalization is not a simple, one-sided matter. All educational procedures need not be highly personalized and in some respects it may be useful to have an impersonal, wholly intellectual educational experience. I am thinking specifically of the fact that either a large impersonal class or an intellectual subject area may provide a respite from personal relationships and concerns. There is no safer place for a freshman to hide and watch the world than from the last row of a lecture class of two hundred students—where he is not apt to be noticed nor have any demands made upon him. By comparison, the degree of exposure inevitable in a small communal experimental program can be frightening.

In the same vein, the idea of losing oneself in one's work— not only in the sense of immersion or engagement but also in a sense of distance from personal encounter—does have merit and should not be lost in the special educational program. The old adage, "absence makes the heart grow fonder," expresses a sound psychological principle which is that distance and closeness define each other and both are needed for either to be important.

Nor is it a simple matter for the teacher to undertake teaching a program that uses the relationship of the student and teacher as the principal process in which the student's development is fostered. Although such a relationship was an important aspect of the ECP, there was no mechanism in the program to aid the teacher —no advice or discussion to prepare him or instruct him: the manner in which he used it, and the extent, depended on his own interest and inclination.

If the ECP and, for that matter, any program of its type, is to provide an opportunity for students to be open to personal scrutiny and evaluation by the faculty, then that opportunity should be used more than as a matter of personal discretion on the part of the teacher. It should be a professional concern of all the faculty together to participate in a careful evaluation of students to maximize the opportunity to know a student's intellectual and developmental needs and to offer guidance as needed. Not that one teacher alone cannot develop a sensitive understanding of a student; I am suggesting that anything that will enhance and expand that understanding will improve the effectiveness of the program. The guidance emerging from a group effort can be used by the one teacher who is currently responsible for a student's individual work and working with him as consultant and mentor.

Considerations such as these, of educational structures and procedures which emphasize working with students individually, have relevance to education generally and are not limited to development of special programs. Consider the matter broadly. People concerned with education at any level are becoming aware that, while teachers may know a great deal about their subject and methods for presenting it, they probably lack knowledge about the individual student or may not even know how to get acquainted with him thus to understand him. Even though the great restlessness and dissatisfaction of students at all educational levels during the last few years can be related to other factors as well, that restlessness is a clear expression of this lack, for one thing. Furthermore, student dissatisfaction demonstrates the lack of understanding of educators in another way: we, the educators, are in profound confusion when responding to student dissatisfaction. Individual teachers, administrators, and schools respond variously; responses range from stands of absolute authority to those of total permissiveness. I am not speaking only of responses to student demonstrations but of resistance to ideas of change and to new programs all the way from first grade to graduate school. Although in some instances there is a willingness to develop new programs which offer students greater opportunity for their individual development, all too often teachers in those programs fundamentally are unchanged, adhering to the same attitudes and values as before and totally unprepared to understand and facilitate any such student development. It happens all too often in the innovative grammar school, for example, that we see the open classroom being taught by a closed teacher. Teachers who are closed to many aspects and questions about life are not the intermediaries needed to insure the success of an innovative program.

Aside from such general consideration, however, I wish• to show the importance of the teacher's knowledge, skills, and understanding vis-a-vis the development of individual students, especially in relation to current changes taking place in higher education. I believe a greater understanding by the teacher of how to discover the uniqueness of individual students with whom he deals—a matter already too long neglected—is a growing necessity brought about because of specific changes in college population and educational programs.

Students entering colleges and universities—especially those in urban centers—are increasingly diverse. There are growing numbers of students from ethnic minority backgrounds: they have special interests, talents, and needs. There are also growing numbers of older students who have had a career of some kind (such as housewives who have raised a family or businessmen whose interests have changed). These mature students either are intent on furthering their knowledge and skills or in embarking in a new direction. There is, furthermore, an increasing desire on the part of all students to put the stamp of their individuality on their college program. They want to design their own major, to substitute work or living experiences for classroom study, or, in the context of the class, to substitute a paper or project in their particular area of interest for the general one assigned.

In various ways many students do not fit into the standard educational programs offered in colleges and universities—defined in terms of four years of general and specialized curriculums—leading toward a degree. Someone from an ethnic minority background may find it difficult to relate his interests and skills to the standard courses and programs; he may have special needs not met by the conventional arrangement. The older student also may be already knowledgeable in some areas beyond the level of training that college can provide and therefore may wish to pick and choose among the curricular requirements. In fact, he or she may be at a level of proficiency that would qualify him to teach some courses.

These changes in students imply that a change in focus is needed in planning programs of general requirements and requirements in areas of major specialization. Where the focus customarily has been on the curriculum, a shift is indicated to redirect focus to the student. Where the body of general knowledge or knowledge in an area of specialization has been the guiding consideration in planning undergraduate programs, the individual student's intellectual development must be given more weight.

My point is that students often cannot make use of a regular, preplanned program. Their need is for teachers with highly de-

veloped talents in perceiving and understanding the individual—
his developmental level, talents, and developmental necessities;
teachers who are as much skilled in looking at a person as they are
experienced and skillful in their scholarly specialty. Teachers are
needed who can adapt the regular program to meet the special
needs of individual students.

Of course, individualization of college programs always has
been possible and often has been accomplished. I am stressing the
fact that more individualized programming is necessary and that
we need to do it by stressing careful consideration of student development rather than by letting it happen casually.

I am not speaking only of what is known as faculty advising
but rather of the whole perspective and orientation of the teacher—
in all his work—being less toward teaching a subject and more
toward teaching students.

Consider still another change that is relevant to this idea
that teachers need to become more skilled in their understanding
of the individual: because of technological development, classroom
teaching is becoming less and less a matter of informing students.
One major change in education at all levels is that information is
being transmitted by mechanical means: programmed instruction
and instruction by videotape are the two most commonly encountered automated teaching devices. (The "external degree," involving
instructional programs on home television is a recent expression of
this technology.) These are the latest developments of an information explosion which has been experienced in technological societies
in the last two decades. As a result of that explosion students often
are well informed in a variety of areas of knowledge but have little
skill in evaluating the information they acquired. Classroom work,
therefore, is increasingly a matter not of informing students but of
helping them sort out what they already know; teaching them to
develop their talents in evaluating knowledge at hand. In this kind
of endeavor an orientation to the individual student and his level of
development is crucial. Experience in a special program emphasizing closer collaboration of student and teacher—such as in the
Experimental College Program—may help a teacher develop such
an outlook as well as the skills necessary to use it in general teaching.

My final reflections concern research on change and the evaluation of experimental educational programs. Especially in my own experience of changing while in the process of doing this study, I became acutely aware of change as a nonlinear process. For example, I experienced occasional flashes of awareness that there was disagreement between our design, which postulated two unitary structures, and our observations, which demonstrated diversity on all sides. At first I resisted that awareness and tried to ignore the discordance, only to be reminded of it again by the emergence of fresh evidence. This cycle was repeated often and in respect to different aspects of the study. It was only when we were considering the work of the final year and different plans came to mind that it became evident that I had changed my views quite basically. The effect was one of a quantum of change, not of gradual change. We observed similar phenomena in the process of change as experienced by both the teachers and the students.

In light of such experiences the measurement of groups by means of personality scales administered at intervals of time seems distinctly limited as a means for studying change occuring in individuals. Yet, as Freedman has aptly demonstrated (1967), this method may have its practical and unique usefulness as a key to understanding social change. Changes in attitudes and values measured by personality scales that may be imperceptible at the individual level can show, in the aggregate, significant shifts in attitudes among succeeding classes of students. Such shifts over time in the campus population may be reflected in significant changes in the behavior of individuals acting in concert.

I propose that the use of personality scales and of the before-and-after measurement be limited to this particular function, and that the study of change be made instead an effort to study change as a process. Such effort should include development of methods for focusing on individuals and on small groups of students. It is particularly important to know the student in various situations in his life at the university so that the continuities and discrepancies in his experiences will be more evident. This can be accomplished by more varied field observations, more intensive interviewing (for example: three successive interviews with the same student in two weeks each semester), and periodic discussions during the semester with small

176 The Best Laid Plans

groups of students who act both as subjects and participant observers for the research. Such methods would allow us to focus on changes in overt behavior and on coincidence of events in the student's life. They would help us observe whether and to what degree such events are harmonious or discrepant and, finally, whether and how the student develops an awareness of the events. We would ask ourselves such questions as when does a student become aware that the professor who once seemed original and exciting becomes outmoded after the student transcends his teacher's ideas? When does the student become aware of having to resolve a tension such as one that develops when he is caught between the conflicting demands of the military training program and the ECP? Is there a discernible point at which such tension becomes critical—when it can be predicted with some degree of safety that a resulting change in action will occur?

Efforts such as these to study the process of change would represent, however, a major new intrusion into the student's life— an intrusion of such magnitude as to be unjustifiable and unwarranted, even for purposes of enhancing research about student development, unless we adopt a different frame of reference. One— and possibly the only—reason that ethically validates such intrusion into the student's personal life is the possibility, or the probability, that he gain from it personally and in an immediate way. It may be possible to combine the functions of student-teacher consultation (such as I already have suggested should be regularly available to the student) and the research function. Whether as a separate research activity or as a part of his academic experience, the student's participation in the research could provide an opportunity for resolving his problems and choices during college, meanwhile providing an opportunity for the researcher to observe the change process at first hand. Thus the student's participation would be to his own immediate and direct benefit. A number of the students in this study clearly made use of the research interviews in this way. I suggest that such a procedure is formalized to the mutual benefit of student, teacher, and researcher.

Finally, I wish to emphasize one other conclusion: a study of change is sorely limited not only by a methodology of measurement over time but also by the method of comparing change agencies; for example, in this study, the two educational programs. The latter method assumes that the programs are internally consistent and comparable. Both methods dictate in advance of the study which variables will be important and thereby limit the likelihood of perceiving and studying other variables which may emerge from the change process. Both methods assume, moreover, the same temporal boundary for the change taking place as for the change agency in which it is expected to occur; that is, that significant change will occur during the period the program is in progress. It may, in fact, occur in another place and another time.

To compare an experimental program with a conventional program—especially in terms of quantitative measures—leads to the anomaly of comparing qualitatively different entities on a quantitative basis. More important, such a comparison is based on the questionable assumption that two qualitatively different experiences can (and perhaps should) be expected to lead to the same quantitatively measurable consequences. I suggest it is time we move this kind of research enterprise from questions of "how much has everyone gained?" to questions of "what is the quality of human life people are living?"

Appendix A

Attitude and
Opinion Survey

*T*his compendium of personality scales consisted of three parts. The first part included six scales taken from the Omnibus Personality Inventory, Form C (Center for Study of Higher Education, 1962): Social Maturity, Impulse Expression, Estheticism, Schizoid Function, Masculinity-Femininity, and Developmental Status. The second part was the Interpersonal Check List (LaForge and Suczek, 1955) used to describe the self. The third part consisted of the Ethnocentrism (E) Scale and the Authoritarianism (F) Scale (Adorno and others, 1950).

None of the results of the Interpersonal Check List are reported in this book, therefore only the other scales are described. All these latter measures were found in previous studies to be sensi-

179

tive to changes experienced by students during the college years (Webster and others, 1962). The following is a brief description of each of the scales.

Social Maturity (SM). A high score may be taken to reflect nonauthoritarianism, flexibility, tolerance, realistic thinking, independence from authority and from rules and rituals, as well as an interest in intellectual and esthetic pursuits.

Impulse Expression (IE). A high score is interpreted as indicating emphasis on sensation, imagination, feelings, and fantasy, as well as readiness to express impulses and to seek gratification either in conscious thought or in overt action.

Schizoid Functioning (SF). A high score indicates social alienation, feelings of isolation, loneliness, rejection, possible avoidance of others, hostility, aggression, identity diffusion, daydreaming, disorientation, feelings of impotence, and fear of loss of control.

Masculinity (MF). A high score indicates interest in problem solving and science rather than in esthetic things and a denial of adjustment problems, as well as a denial of feelings of anxiety and of personal inadequacy.

Estheticism (Es). A high score indicates diverse interests in artistic matters and activities, including art, music, literature, and dramatics.

Developmental Status (DS). A high score indicates attitudes more like those of seniors than those of freshmen, including greater rebelliousness and freedom to express impulses and less authoritarianism.

Ethnocentrism (E). A high score indicates stereotyped negative imagery and hostile attitudes regarding outgroups and stereotyped positive imagery and submissive attitudes regarding ingroups, which are seen as rightly dominant.

Authoritarianism (F). A high score indicates rigid ingroup-outgroup distinctions, stereotypical imagery, dogmatism, intolerance of ambiguity, a stereotyped conception of the importance of authority, and denial of certain needs, such as dependence or weakness.

Appendix B

Readings for the Experimental College Program

During the first year of the ECP the University of California was using a semester system. Readings were assigned for each of the two semesters. During the second year of the ECP the university changed to a quarter system, and, in order to preserve the larger unit of time that had prevailed under the semester system, the first group of readings was assigned for the first two of the three quarters the ECP was to be in session. In the third quarter, devoted to writing of an intellectual biography, a relatively brief list of readings was assigned.

In some instances the faculty chose to use a particular translation or a particular publication of a work (the latter often was one that would cost the students less), and these have been indicated. Otherwise any standard version available was used.

FIRST SEMESTER

HERODOTUS. *The Persian Wars*. Modern Library.
HOMER. *The Iliad*. Lattimore translation. Phoenix.
HOMER. *The Odyssey*. Rieu translation. Penguin.
HESOID. *The Work and Days: Theogony: The Shield of Herakles*. Lattimore translation. University of Michigan Press.
THUCYDIDES. Warner translation. Penguin.
XENOPHON. Rieu translation. University of Michigan Press.
PLUTARCH. *Lives of the Noble Greeks*. Dell Laurel Classics.
PLATO. *Euthyphro, Apology, Crito, Georgias, Phaedo, Republic, Symposium*. Library of Liberal Arts.
SOPHOCLES. *Three Tragedies*. University of Chicago Press.
AESCHYLUS. *Oresteia*. University of Chicago Press.
KITTO, H.D.F. *The Greeks*. Penguin.
ARISTOPHANES. *Complete Plays*.

SECOND SEMESTER

Bible. King James translation.
SHAKESPEARE. *The Histories of Shakespeare*. Complete and unabridged with notes and glossary. Vols. I and II. Modern Library.
SHAKESPEARE. *King Lear, Hamlet*. Signet Classics.
BACON. *Essays of Francis Bacon*. Doubleday Dolphin.
MILTON. *The Portable Milton*. Viking.
HOBBES. *Leviathan*. Everyman.
MACHIAVELLI. *The Prince*. Mentor.
AUBREY, J. *Brief Lives*.
TREVELYAN. Brief history of the seventeenth century.

SECOND YEAR, FIRST AND SECOND QUARTERS

LOCKE, J. *Second Treatise and Letter of Toleration*. Sherman (Ed). Appleton-Century-Crofts.
BURKE. *Reflections on the French Revolution*. Dolphin.

PAINE. *Rights of Man*. Dolphin.

ADAMS, H. *United States in 1800*.

MADISON, HAMILTON, AND JAY. *The Federalist Papers*. Meridian Books.

KENYON, C. M. *The Anti-Federalist*. Bobbs-Merrill.

SOLBERG. *The Federal Convention and Formation of Union*. Bobbs-Merrill.

TUSSMAN, J. *Supreme Court on Church and State, Supreme Court on Racial Discrimination*. Oxford.

MEIKLEJOHN, A. *Political Freedom*. Oxford.

MEIKLEJOHN, A. *Education Between Two Worlds*.

DE TOCQUEVILLE. *Democracy in America*. 2 vols. Vintage.

SECOND YEAR, THIRD QUARTER

DOSTOYEVSKY. *The Brothers Karamazov*. Magarshack translation.

JOYCE. *Ulysses*.

ADAMS, H. *The Education of Henry Adams*.

Appendix C

Classification
of Development

Procedures referred to in Chapter
Six which were used to classify students as "developed" or "not
developed" were based on five measures: the Authoritarianism and
Ethnocentrism scales (Adorno and others, 1950) and the Social
Maturity-, Impulse Expression-, and Estheticism scales contained
in the Omnibus Personality Inventory (Center for the Study of
Higher Education, 1962).

The first procedure for classifying students used the pattern
of separate scale scores to identify development. Students were classified as developed if their standard scores on Social Maturity, Impulse Expression, and Estheticism increased—that is, if standard
scores on two of these scales increased by at least five points between

the first and second testing and if the score on the third scale did not decrease five or more points. Students were considered as non-developed if their scores decreased by five or more points on one of the three scales and did not increase five or more points on either of the other two. Students who did not fall into these two classes were judged developed if their scores decreased five or more points on both the Authoritarianism and Ethnocentrism scales or fifteen points on Authoritarianism alone, and they were classified as non-developed if their standard scores on both those scales increased by five points or more or by ten points on either one of the two scales.

Some students began at a more complex stage of development than others and scored high on the Social Maturity and Impulse Expression scales at the time they entered; consequently they had less possibility of increasing their scores. Therefore, students who had scored in the highest quartile on these two measures at the start were considered developed even if they showed no increase. They were classified as nondeveloped if their standard scores on Social Maturity or Impulse Expression fell below the average, to forty-five or less, or if their standard scores on Authoritarianism rose fifteen points. They were also considered nondeveloped if their Impulse Expression score rose to over 65 since extremely high scores on this scale suggest inflexibility in self-control. In brief, these classifications include consideration of development characterized by impulsive, uncontrolled behavior being brought under flexible control.

The second method used for classification used scores—initial test scores and scores on the retesting—which had been converted (each testing separately) to standard scores with a mean of 50 and a standard deviation of 10. The individual's five scores were expressed as deviations from the mean, so that they were comparable and could be averaged. By averaging the five mean scores, we gave each individual a general complexity score for the first and for the later testing.

References

ADORNO, T. W., FRENKEL-BRUNSWICK, E., LEVINSON, D., AND SANFORD, N. *The Authoritarian Personality*. New York: Harper and Row, 1950.

ALFERT, E. AND SUCZEK, R. F. "Personality Development and Cultural Change." *Journal of Higher Education*, 1971, *42*(1).

ALLPORT, G. *The Nature of Prejudice*. Reading, Mass.: Addison-Wesley, 1954.

AXELROD, J., FREEDMAN, M. B., HATCH, W. R., KATZ, J., AND SANFORD, N. *Search for Relevance*. San Francisco: Jossey-Bass, 1969.

CARLSON, H. B. "Attitudes of Undergraduate Students." *Journal of Social Psychology*, 1934, *5*, 202–242.

Carnegie Commission on Higher Education. *Less Time, More Options*. New York: McGraw Hill, 1971.

CARROLL, L. *Alice in Wonderland and Through the Looking Glass*. New York: Grosset and Dunlap, 1946.

Center for Study of Higher Education, University of California. *Omnibus Personality Inventory: Research Manual.* Berkeley, 1962.

CHICKERING, A. W. *Education and Identity.* San Francisco: Jossey-Bass, 1971.

DEWEY, JOHN. *Experience and Nature.* New York: Dover Books, 1958.

ERIKSON, E. H. *Childhood and Society.* New York: Norton, 1950.

FELDMAN, K. A., AND NEWCOMB, T. M. *The Impact of College on Students.* San Francisco: Jossey-Bass, 1969.

FRANK, L. K. *On the Importance of Infancy.* New York: Random House, 1966.

FREEDMAN, M. B. *The College Experience.* San Francisco: Jossey-Bass, 1967.

GAFF, J. (Ed.), *The Cluster College.* San Francisco: Jossey-Bass, 1970.

GOFFMAN, E. *The Presentation of Self in Everyday Life.* New York: Doubleday Anchor Books, 1959.

HAAN, N., SMITH, M. B., AND BLOCK, J. "Moral Reasoning of Young Adults: Political-Social Behavior, Family Background, and Personality Correlates." *Journal of Personality and Social Psychology,* 1968, *10,* 183–201.

HARRIS, A. J., REMMERS, H. H., AND ELLISON, C. E. "The Relation Between Liberal and Conservative Attitudes in College Students and Other Factors." *Journal of Social Psychology,* 1932, *3,* 320–335.

HEIST, P., MC CONNELL, T. R., MATSLER, F., AND WILLIAMS, P. "Personality and Scholarship." *Science,* 1961, *133* (3450), 362–367.

HEIST, P., AND WEBSTER, H. "Differential Characteristics of Student Bodies—Implications for the Selection and Study of Undergraduates." In *Selection and Educational Differentiation.* Berkeley: Center for the Study of Higher Education, 1959.

KATZ, J., AND ASSOCIATES. *No Time for Youth.* San Francisco: Jossey-Bass, 1968.

LA FORGE, R., AND SUCZEK, R. "The Interpersonal Dimension of Personality III: An Interpersonal Check List." *Journal of Personality,* 1955, *24*(1).

MASLOW, A. H., AND SAKODA, J. M. "Volunteer-Error in the Kinsey Report." *Journal of Abnormal and Social Psychology.* 1952, 47(2), 259–262.

MC LUHAN, M. *The Medium is the Massage.* New York: Bantam Books, 1967.

MEAD, G. H. *On Social Psychology.* Anselm Strauss (Ed.). Chicago: University of Chicago Press, 1964.

MEDAWAR, P. "Facts and Fiction about Scientific Method." Mc-Enerny Lectures, University of California, Berkeley, 1966–1967.

MEIKLEJOHN, A. *The Experimental College.* New York: Harper and Brothers, 1932.

NEWCOMB, T. M. *Personality and Social Change.* New York: Holt, 1943.

NEWCOMB, T. M., BROWN, D. R., KULIK, J., REIMER, D. J., AND REVELLE, W. R. "Self Selection and Change." In J. Gaff (Ed.), *Cluster Colleges.* San Francisco: Jossey-Bass, 1970.

PLANT, W. T. "Longitudinal Changes in Intolerance and Authoritarianism for Subjects Differing in Amount of College Education Over Four Years." *Genetic Psychology Monographs,* 1965, 72, 247–287.

PLANT, W. T., AND TELFORD, C. W. "Changes in Personality for Groups Completing Different Amounts of College Over Two Years." *Genetic Psychology Monographs,* 1966, 74, 3–36.

REISMAN, D. "The Uncommitted Generation." *Encounter,* 1960, 15, 25–30.

REISMAN, D. WITH GLAZER, N., AND DENNEY, R. *The Lonely Crowd.* New Haven: Yale University Press, 1950.

ROE, A. A Psychological Study of Eminent Psychologists. *Psychological Monographs, General and Applied.* American Psychological Association, 1953, 67(2).

ROSCOE, J. T. Religious Beliefs of American College Students. *College Student Survey,* 1968, 2, 49–55.

SANFORD, N. "A Psychologist's View of Individual Development in the Years After College." Commencement address, University of Richmond, June 11, 1962a.

SANFORD, N. "Developmental Status of the Entering Freshman." In

N. Sanford (Ed.), *The American College*. New York: Wiley, 1962b, 253–282.

SANFORD, N. (Ed.) *The American College*. New York: Wiley, 1962.

SANFORD, N. *Self and Society*. New York: Atherton Press, 1966.

SANFORD, N. *Where Colleges Fail*. San Francisco: Jossey-Bass, 1967.

SAVIO, M. Speech to Free Speech Movement Rally, December 2, 1964. Quoted in *The Daily Californian*, June 30, 1967, p. 12.

STRAUSS, A. L. *Mirrors and Masks*. San Francisco: The Sociology Press, 1969.

SUCZEK, R. Self Selection and Special Educational Programs. *Journal of Higher Education*, 1970, in press.

SUCZEK, R., AND ALFERT, E. *Personality Characteristics of College Dropouts*. Washington, D.C.: Educational Research Information Center, 1965.

SUCZEK, R. AND ALFERT, E. "Personality Development in Two Different Educational Atmospheres." U.S. Department of Health, Education, and Welfare Project 6-1293. Berkeley: Department of Psychiatry, Student Health Service, University of California, 1970.

TRENT, J. W., AND MEDSKER, L. L. *Beyond High School*. San Francisco: Jossey-Bass, 1968.

TUSSMAN, J. *Obligation and the Body Politic*. New York: Oxford University Press, 1960.

TUSSMAN, J. "The Experimental Program and the University." *The Daily Californian*, Oct. 12, 1967.

TUSSMAN, J. *Experiment at Berkeley*. New York: Oxford, 1969.

Voice of Troy. DelValle High School, Walnut Creek, California. January 23, 1969.

WEBSTER, H., FREEDMAN, M., AND HEIST, P. "Personality Changes in College Students." In N. Sanford (Ed.), *The American College*. New York: Wiley, 1962, 811–846.

WHEELIS, A. "The Place of Action in Personality Change." *Psychiatry*, 1950, *13*(2).

WHEELIS, A. "How People Change." *Commentary*, 1969, *47*, (5).

WILLEMS, E. P., AND RAUSH, H. L. *Naturalistic Viewpoints in Psychological Research*. New York: Holt, Rinehart, and Winston, 1969.

Index